*With Sincere Thanks and Happy Holiday Wishes
from Taylor Porter*

In recognition of Taylor Porter's valued relationship with you, we are pleased to share an autographed copy of *Jay Ducote's Louisiana Outdoor Cooking*.

Featuring more than 150 recipes suitable for any outdoor activity, the cookbook emphasizes Louisiana celebrity chef Jay Ducote's love of food and local culture.

Ducote's career began in college when he cooked under the oak trees on the LSU campus prior to football games. Over the years, his popular tailgate parties have showcased Cajun favorites, such as chicken and andouille gumbo, crawfish hushpuppies, grilled shrimp, jambalaya and much more. Now a popular radio host, caterer, and restaurant owner, Ducote's *Bite & Booze* radio show has received a Taste Award for Best Food or Drink Radio Broadcast as well as the Uniquely Louisiana Award from the Louisiana Association of Broadcasters. We hope you will enjoy the culinary contributions to Louisiana's culture found in his cookbook.

2020 has presented unprecedented challenges. Taylor Porter is proud and grateful to have had the opportunity to join with you in meeting these challenges. The entire Taylor Porter family values its relationship with our valued clients and colleagues, and remains committed to working to achieve the best outcomes for you and your business.

Happy Holidays to you and your families!

TAYLOR PORTER
LOUISIANA'S LAW FIRM®

SINCE 1912

# JAY DUCOTE'S
# LOUISIANA OUTDOOR COOKING

# JAY DU

# LOUISIANA OUT

## ~ WITH CYNTHIA

# COTE'S

# DOOR COOKING

## JEUNE NOBLES ~

Louisiana State University Press / Baton Rouge

Published with the assistance of the Borne Fund

Published by Louisiana State University Press
www.lsupress.org

Manufactured in Canada
First printing

Designer: Michelle A. Neustrom
Typeface: Sentinel
Printer and binder: Friesens Corporation

Photograph of author on front cover courtesy Jenn Ocken Photography.
All other photographs on front and back covers courtesy Jordan Hefler
Photography. Used with permission of Jay Ducote.

Library of Congress Cataloging-in-Publication Data

Names: Ducote, Jay, author. | Nobles, Cynthia LeJeune, 1954–, author.
Title: Jay Ducote's Louisiana outdoor cooking / Jay Ducote, with
    Cynthia LeJeune Nobles.
Description: Baton Rouge : Louisiana State University Press, [2020] |
    Includes index.
Identifiers: LCCN 2020005555 | ISBN 978-0-8071-7296-4 (cloth)
Subjects: LCSH: Cooking, American—Louisiana style. | Cooking—
    Louisiana—New Orleans. | Outdoor cooking—Louisiana. | LCGFT:
    Cookbooks.
Classification: LCC TX715.2.L68 D83 2020 | DDC 641.59763—dc23
LC record available at https://lccn.loc.gov/2020005555

# CONTENTS

# FOREWORD

We still remember the college-aged Jay Ducote on football game days, standing outside of Tiger Stadium wearing his LSU shirt and with tongs in hand. His crowded patch of grass was his happy place, and the set of tongs was his tool for creating happiness for other people. As a young cook, you don't exactly know why you love to crank up the fires and get grilling; you just do it. But as you grow as a chef, as Jay has done spectacularly, the reasons become evident. You put in the hours and stir the jambalaya for the joy of putting a smile on someone's face with your food. Then, after the plates are clean, you hang around for the compliments and conversations.

Jay is the perfect example of the joy found in the culinary world, and he completely amplifies every aspect of it. With a food blog, radio show, numerous national TV appearances, and awards, as well as his own line of food and beverage products, his enthusiasm shows no sign of slowing down. Every time we get the privilege of cooking with him, he has a bigger smile and enjoyment for what he does. He's also an extremely impactful speaker with the goal of making people fall in love with Louisiana cooking. He uses this knowledge and talent to teach cooks to create their own amazing dishes, all while inspiring them to think outside the culinary box.

When we first cooked at the James Beard House in New York, Jay showed up to help—and mostly to eat. He also seemed almost as excited as we were to be in that legendary kitchen. The night before we prepared our dinner, we took him with us to Blue Hill at Stone Barns, a Hudson Valley restaurant that serves food from its surrounding fields and pastures. While we enjoyed a multicourse dinner paired with world-renowned wines, we could see the passion Jay carried for everything he ate and drank. That's when it hit us: this guy really loves food! A year later he was cooking his own dinner at the Beard House, modeling his menu after the dishes he had cooked at LSU tailgate parties, as well as the ones he created on *Food Network Star*.

When it comes to tailgate parties, there's no better expert or representative than Jay. It's always a highlight of pre-football festivities to see him on LSU's campus, whether he's cooking, going around with a camera crew, or just drinking a beer with his friends. We'll never forget the time he cooked outside the stadium as the featured chef on ESPN's *College GameDay*. That day Jay brought his A-game, laying out a spread of whole grilled red snapper, char-grilled oysters, sausage, boudin, ribs, and things we can't even remember. From our own tailgate party, we watched it all unfold on TV. Then, sure enough, a few hours later Jay walked clear across campus to our tailgate party, shadowed by national food writer Naomi Tomky, who followed him around to write a story. Tomky wanted to see a "cochon-de-elephant," and we had one roasting. This specialty is a whole pig dressed to look like a small elephant, using pork tenderloin for a trunk and pork chops for ears. This rival-driven creation only comes out every two years, when LSU plays host to Alabama. Tomky was obviously impressed with our suckling pig, and it made the story in Vice Media's food blog, *Munchies*.

And that takes us to this cookbook, which will become your go-to tool for every backyard barbecue, outdoor party, and tailgate you'll host. Jay's love for south Louisiana cooking is this book's backbone. He will spur your creativity to try new things, and he will inspire you to have a good time doing it. The limitless smells, sounds, and flavors of cooking outdoors are just some of the things that make what he does so captivating. Jay is widely known for putting a smile on people's faces, and this book will definitely do the same.

**Chefs Cody and Samantha Carroll**

# PREFACE

Outdoor cooking is my first real memory of food. Even before I was big enough to hold up a shotgun, I tagged along to our family's Avoyelles Parish, Louisiana, hunting camp in the middle of the woods. Home base was a rustic two-story cabin built by my grandfather and his sons, and dinner there could be cooked on an antique wood-burning stove or, more often, on an outdoor grill. I was born in Baton Rouge, but by the time I was old enough to hunt with my dad, our family had moved to Sugar Land, Texas, outside of Houston. While there, we spent a lot of time at south Texas deer camps, where meals were often charred over open mesquite fires.

I'm now back in Baton Rouge, where I'm a chef, caterer, writer, speaker, entertainer, and hugger, as well as a radio host, blogger, video producer, adult beverage enthusiast, and professional tailgater. I also travel a lot, and I'll go just about anywhere for food that tastes exceptional, especially if it's cooked outside.

My blog and radio show are aptly called *Bite & Booze,* and it was my blog that inspired this cookbook, a collection of recipes that I've been testing, refining, and cooking for my family, my friends, and my customers for years. When I'm not writing about food, I'm talking about it, or I'm cooking at my restaurant, Gov't Taco, or at an offsite event. When I have downtime, I'm at my Baton Rouge headquarters, where I experiment with recipes, constantly figuring out how to make our delicious traditional flavors taste extraordinary.

There's very little food I don't like. Thinking about it, probably the only thing I won't eat is pickles. As a child I could never stomach pickles or relish, and my disdain for them is so great that some of my friends created the cartoonish character of Pickle Man to serve as my archnemesis. On the other hand, my absolute favorite things to eat are those that have been thrown on a fiery grill or slow-cooked in a smoker. Smoke, however, adds only one layer of seasoning.

In addition to adding flavor using the right cooking technique, it's important to add herbs and spices throughout the cooking process. My appreciation

Jay grilling his freshman year.

for seasoning came from my two Louisiana-born grandmothers, Maw Maw and Granny. I'll never forget the scents that came out of their kitchens: the nutty roux flavor of gumbo, the peppery tang of étouffée, and the earthy smell of a stew made from whatever my father brought home from a hunt. Maw Maw's cuisine was pure Cajun. Granny's tastes were more continental, and she dabbled with any kind of recipe. Baking, in particular, struck her fancy. But although these two ladies certainly had different cooking styles, both instinctively knew how to season properly and to turn any dish into a culinary masterpiece.

I was in college when I learned that if I wanted to eat well all the time, not just at a restaurant or at my grandmothers' houses, I had to learn how to cook. My introduction to cooking was unorthodox—I earned my culinary stripes outside the gates of Tiger Stadium at LSU. At my first football game in the fall of 1999, my cousin Travis handed me our grandfather's old barbecue tools and said, "Here Freshman, you're in charge of the grill now." It's been trial by fire ever since. For a full decade, at every home game, I took charge of a mishmash of charcoal grills, wood smokers, gigantic pots, and cast-iron cauldrons. With the help of Travis and a few buddies, I'd churn out barbecue, jambalaya, gumbo, fried catfish, boudin balls, hushpuppies, and red beans and rice—anything Cajun—and serve it to up to several hundred friends and fellow Tiger fans. To some, that might sound like work. To me, it was pure joy.

As much as I loved cooking at those football games, I never thought I'd end up in the food business. Eventually, I graduated from LSU, first with a bachelor's degree in political science and economics, then again with a master's degree, also in political science, which isn't exactly a requirement for success in the culinary arts. I did, however, learn that I didn't want to have anything to do with politics. Graduating and leaving campus was bittersweet. I looked forward to making my way on my own, but I have to admit, for me college was an adventure, and I didn't want those carefree days to end. So, on second thought, I decided maybe the tailgating wouldn't have to go, and all I needed until I found my life's calling was beer money for another football season. My good friend Brent, a fellow tailgating buddy, had the same aspiration. He convinced me that something part-time would cover our Saturday night expenses, so we applied to be substitute teachers with the East Baton Rouge Parish School System.

It was only two days before the beginning of the semester, and we were both sent to interview with Lee High School. They were short of teachers, and we ended up getting hired on with full-time teaching jobs. Brent taught algebra and geometry. I taught financial math and algebra to students who had not passed previously. Teaching turned out to be extremely rewarding. My mom was an educator, and I once entertained the thought of getting my PhD and becoming a college professor. At Lee High, I enjoyed interacting with the students, especially when I coached the school's baseball team. The kids sort of took to me, too, because in both the classroom and on the field I was often looked upon as a positive male role model. I quickly learned, however, that repetitive work, the bureaucracy of public education, and grading papers weren't for me. After two years, Lee High closed, and I decided not to pursue a teaching position at another school. Brent, I'm proud to say, found his niche and stuck with education all the way to serving as the dean of students at Baton Rouge's Woodlawn High School.

A short while after I stopped teaching, while on a trip to catch a few Cubs games in Chicago and to tour breweries in Milwaukee, I received an email from a former professor that the Louisiana Department of Health and Hospitals was looking for a researcher and grant writer. I applied and I ended up with the position. I actually thought this might be my dream job. I enjoy reading great books and writing. How different could those interests be from doing research and grant writing? Unfortunately, business writing is not the same as Tolkien or my favorite author, that great philosopher Dr. Seuss. Worse, I had to spend my days cooped up in a cubicle at a computer desk, and I once again found myself going through the mundane motions of bureaucracy.

To prevent midday napping at my desk, I wrote detailed accounts about the lunches I'd been enjoying in downtown Baton Rouge. Soon I had pages and pages of notes. To be sure my growing food journal didn't go stale, I sought out every little restaurant around, making sure I ordered something different for each meal. This all started at the same time that social media really took off. Determined to jump into the world of blogging, I figured out (mostly) what blogs were all about, and I dubbed my website and social media accounts *Bite & Booze*. My lunchtime journals and tailgate stories were now featured on the Internet. Then something interesting happened. Over a short period of time, my restaurant critiques and food reviews turned into something that people wanted to read. I was more shocked than anyone that the blog caught on, and that I was also eagerly keeping it current and interesting.

So I became a serious food blogger. To upgrade my cooking skills, I kept reading and experimenting. I also kept hosting humongous tailgate parties, which

**The Ducote family tailgating.**

was a hands-on education I couldn't have received at any school. To keep my blog focused, I decided to center everything on the cuisine of Louisiana, in addition to anything else I ate and drank while I traveled. Our Cajun dishes are some of the best in the world, and they also have unique histories. I wanted to write about it all, with the hope of getting my generation interested in cooking not only faddish foods, but also the time-honored dishes of their grandparents.

Before I knew it, my *Bite & Booze* presence on the Internet led to my award-winning radio show. Then I started a successful catering and pop-up business, along with a line of food products. (A pop-up is an informal party that's typically hosted in an unexpected location.) I opened my restaurant, Gov't Taco, and I've cooked at the James Beard House twice and have made several appearances on national television. I even received the honor of being runner-up in season 11 of *Food Network Star*, and in 2019, I won an episode of *Beat Bobby Flay* in the celebrity chef's own kitchen.

All this cooking has generated a large collection of personal recipes. In these pages you'll find tweaked and refined versions of many of my most popular dishes, as well as a large selection that comes from a pile I've been tinkering with for years. Most of my recipes were created for cooking outdoors, but many of them can be prepared on your home stove. I give instructions for using both cooking methods. I also include recipes for my commercial brands of sauces and seasoning rubs. Several recipes call for them, and if you can't get your hands on what I sell, you can make your own with extremely close results.

So here I am now, a culinary personality and Louisiana food ambassador with a cookbook that tells my life story. As you browse through it, you'll find that I mostly spend my days stirring pots, traveling, and promoting the culture and cuisine of south Louisiana. I never tire of talking about Cajun food and the boozy beverages we wash it all down with. To me, every day is a holiday, especially when it's spent cooking and sipping a cold one in the great outdoors.

**Jay on *Beat Bobby Flay*.**

# ACKNOWLEDGMENTS

This book has been in the works for years with no manuscript, just a dream from a young man trying to find a way in the culinary world. I'd like to start by thanking LSU Press for sticking with me, and to Louisiana State University for believing in me as a Tiger. From two degrees and tailgate parties to some of the biggest things that have happened to me, including taking the stage for TEDx-LSU and giving a commencement speech, LSU has been a huge part of my life, and I'm honored to work with the Press on my first book. Also, thanks to Cynthia Nobles for having faith in me and spending countless hours helping me with this manuscript, testing recipes, organizing my thoughts, and transcribing my stories. This book wouldn't have been possible without you, Cynthia.

I'd like to thank my immediate family. Mom and Dad, thanks for allowing me the opportunity to chase my dreams, encouraging my tailgate exploits, and cheering me on along the way. This book is for Maw Maw and Granny. The smells that came from the kitchens that my parents grew up in still inspire my food dreams today. To Dana, Eric, and Mandi, thanks for being my biggest fans, there to cheer me on during Food Network shows or to simply buy a taco; your support is always so special.

To my cousin Travis, thanks for putting our grandfather's old barbecue utensils in my hands during my first season of tailgating at that Natatorium. That moment set off a chain reaction that hasn't slowed down. I remember all the nights of cooking sausage with rice and gravy and the lengths we went through to improve our tailgate party year after year.

Eusebio Gongora, in our college days, who would have ever thought that we'd wind up on this kind of culinary journey together? You were my teacher before I ever had a clue what I was even trying to do, and your wisdom still helps me today. It was an honor to be the Best Man in your wedding, and you are definitely the best friend a guy could ask for.

Before I got into the food world, I taught high school with Brent Broussard. Before we taught high school and coached baseball together, we tailgated.

Hard. Brent, thanks for all the memories. Thanks for the road trips, the guy trips, the adventures past and journeys still to come. I have no clue what path my life would have taken had we not accepted those math teacher positions together. And to think, all we really wanted was beer money for the 2007 football season. I mean, we did win a National Championship that year. And also, thanks for the continued support for all of my endeavors. You're always there to lend a hand when I need you, and as my summer manager, I'll tell my boss you need a raise.

In this crazy culinary world, perhaps one of the biggest difference makers has been Tommy Talley. Tommy, from the moment you first pointed a camera at me, something stuck. I would have never dreamed of doing all the video, TV, radio, and other media things that I'm doing now had we not spent hours in edit bays together with you showing me the ropes. Those early projects that we did laid the groundwork for all of this. But even more than the professional accomplishments, I take pride in our friendship, and of course our fantasy baseball victories.

To Blair Loup, my first employee, when I didn't know if I could afford one, who has stuck by my side through everything. Thank you for your unwavering loyalty, passion, and personality. There's no telling where I'd be right now had you not come into my life at the exact right time. From the early days of making barbecue sauce in crawfish pots under my carport to leading a multifaceted culinary monster of an organization, your endless enthusiasm keeps me going.

Chuck P, from that first podcast we did together I could tell that you were my kind of dude. Always there for me, always having my back, always stepping up to represent my brands in the way that I'd want to do it myself. Nobody can ever question the size of your heart and the warmth of your spirit. Thanks for producing my radio show, growing my product line, drinking countless beers, and drooling over burgers with me.

For Therese Albornoz, the rest of the Gov't Taco team, and everyone who has come through our organization, thanks for all the hard work and dedication to building something for the people and by the people. Therese, you've led that brigade better than anyone I could have hired for that job, and we're not done yet. Thanks for rocking the world as my culinary director and bringing your skills and flavors to life in so many kitchens!

To Flynn Foster, Forrest Mills, Gordy Rush, Brian Rodriguez, and the entire team at Guaranty, it's such an honor to be a part of your family. I'm even more excited about the next ten years than I am about the past decade.

And finally to Paul Arrigo. You're responsible for all this. Thank you.

# JAY DUCOTE'S
# LOUISIANA OUTDOOR COOKING

Cooking outdoors.

# BEGINNINGS

When Louisianans throw a party, the festivities often revolve around something cooked outdoors. I guess we're following in the footsteps of our colonial era ancestors. Their houses had few indoor cooking facilities, if any at all, and in the semitropical climate of Baton Rouge, where I live, the natural thing to do was to barbecue and stir hot kettles under the trees.

Today, even with fully furnished and air-conditioned kitchens, we still like to entertain in the backyard around boiling pots and smoking fires. Modern menus might include grilled steaks or pork chops, or perhaps smoked ribs. Sometimes it's fried catfish or speckled trout, or maybe boiled crabs or shrimp. In the springtime, of course, there's always crawfish, and in the winter, venison and wild duck.

For me, cooking outside, even under challenging conditions, is fun. I don't care if the mosquitoes are swarming and the temperature is soaring, or if I'm catering for hundreds or alone with a single bone-in rib eye; cooking outdoors always feels like a celebration, especially with a cold beer in my hand.

No matter how or where it's prepared, I've always had a reverence for great-tasting food, which seems typical of most Cajuns. First, let me clear up something: Creole and Cajun foods are not the same thing. The original Creoles were the people born to settlers in French Colonial Louisiana before the Louisiana Purchase in 1803. These were mostly city dwellers, in New Orleans, and their traditional style of cooking included sophisticated stocks and sauces, and it was relatively refined. Over time, this food adapted with influences from Africa, the Caribbean, and from European countries, such as Italy, Spain, and Germany. The Cajuns, originally known as Acadians, were the French-speaking farmers and fishermen who were kicked out of Nova Scotia by the English in the 1700s. A large number of those who were displaced settled in the swamps and prairies of south Louisiana, where they scratched out livings by farming, fishing, trapping, and hunting. Louisiana's Cajun region, also called Acadiana, is known for its rustic, deeply flavored smoked and one-pot dishes.

**Jay with his parents, Phyllis and Jere, at LSU graduation, May 2004.**

Baton Rouge has the interesting distinction of being the crossroads where Cajun, Creole, and traditional southern meet. It's Louisiana's capital city and a university town, and it's a true cultural melting pot.

My love of Louisiana's food and just about anything else edible followed me to Texas, where my family lived during most of my elementary and high school years. Texas, by the way, is another state that loves to barbecue, and during that time away, the Ducote clan certainly did our share of grilling. But for virtually every holiday, we drove back to our relatives in Louisiana, where our typical Thanksgiving and Christmas dinners were held in a grandmother's house that overflowed with family. As soon as we'd reach Baton Rouge, my mom usually insisted that we stop by Tony's, an iconic local seafood market, to pick up boudin balls and boiled seafood. At my grandmothers' homes, the stoves and tables would be filled with more food than the bustling crowd could devour. Maw Maw's holiday house, in particular, was often bursting at the seams, and in the midst of all the excitement, she'd fry fish in her seasoned cast-iron skillet or stir the roux for chicken and sausage gumbo. When I was about eighteen, we moved back to Baton Rouge permanently. Throughout my college years, Granny, who was best known for her roasts, stews, and cakes, cooked for my family every Sunday.

It was at my grandmothers' houses and at a hunting camp my grandfather built that I received my first kernels of cooking education. Even though I'm not a classically trained chef, I am a nitty-gritty cook who knows what good food tastes like, and I credit my love and knowledge of food to my grandmothers. Through early adulthood, I was soaking in their knowledge of seasoning, basting, browning, grilling, carving, and serving. I listened intently when they talked about Louisiana's vibrant food traditions and the proper way to cook our classic dishes. Little did I know that one day I'd inherit some of the old recipes, canisters, and pots that made their kitchens sing. I never imagined that their inspiration would lead me to a career in cooking, and that their stories and culinary wisdom would be the basis for a radio show that tells the world about my favorite subject, food.

## The Birth of *Bite & Booze*

When I'm outside stirring pots or flipping something on a grill, I almost always have an adult beverage in hand. There's something about sipping a cold one and watching smoke drift up from a barbecue pit; it makes me feel that all is right with the world. I wasn't always particular about my beer, and all through college I drank just about anything. These days, however, I have a special appreciation for beers that are locally crafted. And aside from pickles, which I think are a waste of perfectly good cucumbers, I eat just about anything. So, when I was looking for a name for my blog in 2009, I combined my two gustatory interests and came up with *Bite & Booze.*

I created my blog a few years after I graduated from Louisiana State University. This was right after I had taught for two years in a local high school and had just ended a decade-long stint cooking outside Tiger Stadium before every home game for masses of hungry football-crazy fans. (More on that in the next chapter.) At the time, I was grant writing for the state of Louisiana. Bored with real work, I began writing about local restaurants, as well as my tailgate recipes and my exploration of a recently invigorated local craft-beer industry. In those early days, my blog got a surprising number of hits, but I wanted to make it more interesting, so I collaborated with my friend Tommy Talley to produce video content and incorporate that into my web posts. Tommy was a buddy from LSU, and he'd just moved from Los Angeles back to Baton Rouge to open his own digital media company. We worked together and came up with food videos, which were mostly me on camera eating and drinking and talking about food. The videos were a hit, and fan responses told me that there was a demand for more.

Okay, I admit it. While I was a grant writer for the state of Louisiana, I spent some of that time clandestinely building up my blog. In early 2011 I took an even more daring step, when I learned that the Baton Rouge radio station 107.3 FM was turning into an all-talk station, and they were looking to fill weekend time slots with programming that was local and nonpolitical. I sent them an email about my tailgate cooking, my blog, and my love of food, along with a few video clips. The next day I was invited to their office to discuss the idea of the *Bite & Booze Radio Show.* My show began airing in April of 2011. By that August, I had quit my government job to pursue the culinary world full-time.

I guess there is a need for new and different talk shows, because the *Bite & Booze Radio Show* started out with a one-hour broadcast and then quickly grew into a two-hour show. My guests and I have lively discussions about local food trends, food events, and the south Louisiana restaurant scene. We discuss what's fresh at farmers' markets, who's publishing new cookbooks, who's growing, brewing, and distilling, and what I'm cooking and where. I'm going out on a large limb here and saying that Louisiana has the most important, eclectic,

In 2014, Jay Ducote's *Bite & Booze* radio show won the national Taste Award for Best Food or Drink Radio Broadcast. The annual awards, also known as the Tasty Awards, highlight food, fashion, home, and lifestyle programs from television, film, online, radio, and live interactive events. The *Bite & Booze Radio Show* also won the Uniquely Louisiana Award from the Louisiana Association of Broadcasters in 2015 for Jay's work celebrating, preserving, and promoting Louisiana's culture through broadcast content.

colorful, unique, multicultural, and appetizing food culture in the United States. I'm passionate about preserving and passing on our food stories, and one way I do that is talking about it on the radio.

My good buddy and the show's producer, Charles Pierce, or Chuck P as we call him, has been with me from nearly the start. Charles, a beer-and-burger aficionado, gets particularly enthused when we do our regular segments called "On Tap," which is all about beer, and "Booze Block," which is a discussion of what's happening in the worlds of wine, spirits, and cocktails.

It's pretty easy to get a discussion going about locally crafted beers. Louisiana boasts some of the nation's finest brews, and they're being made all over. In Acadiana there's Parish Brewing Company, Bayou Teche Brewery, Wheel Brewery, and Crying Eagle Brewing. North of Lake Pontchartrain is Chafunkta Brewing Company, Old Rail Brewing, and Gnarly Barley. Among this group is Abita Brewing Company, the pioneer that started craft brewing in Louisiana back in 1986.

New Orleans, which was the largest beer-producing city in the South before Prohibition, has Urban South Brewing, NOLA Brewing Company, Miel Brewing, Courtyard Brewery, Port Orleans Brewing, and Parleaux Beer Lab, to name a few. Even the more conservative region of north Louisiana has an impressive number, including Great Raft Brewing, Red River Brewing, Flying Tiger Brewing, Flying Heart Brewing, and several others. Southern Craft Brewing is in Baton Rouge, as is Tin Roof Brewing, where I do a lot of pop-ups. Tin Roof, which launched around the same time I started my blog and radio show, has actually been one of my commercial partners from the beginning.

I'm proud to say I've visited almost all of the more than thirty, and counting, breweries in Louisiana. Each has its own way of doing things, and their products can stand up to or exceed what's made by national brands. On my radio show I use a good chunk of airtime debating the nuances of locally crafted beers. Hopefully, I'm playing a small part to help our brewers spread their good news. I think I owe it to them. Their products are, after all, a big part of what inspired me to create my *Bite & Booze* blog and radio show.

## Growing My Cooking Arsenal

If you listen to my radio show or follow my social media at all, you know that I'm often outdoors grilling, frying, boiling, smoking, and smothering something delicious for large groups of people. And regardless of what's on the menu, success depends on having the proper equipment.

**Jay grilling at Tin Roof Brewing.**

Jay with the "Monstrosity."

If you're fortunate enough to cook outside for a crowd often, then you have the excuse to buy things like propane burners, crawfish pots, and offset smokers, the culinary gear you need to power you through. These implements are common here in Baton Rouge, where many homeowners often have decent-sized patios or yards equipped with at least a nice grill. Many homes, especially in rural parts of south Louisiana, have fully equipped outdoor kitchens.

I have a large collection of pots and culinary gadgets, but it wasn't always that way. My serious outdoor cooking began with a single Weber kettle grill. I began what would eventually become my career on a student budget, cooking at LSU tailgate parties. Early on, the little kettle-style pit certainly did the job, but as demand for my game-day food exploded, I needed something larger, and I needed multiple ways to cook. To solve my barbecue-pit problem, my cousin Travis, our tailgate buddy Matt, and I skipped a couple of days of school to weld together an all-in-one charcoal-and-wood grill and smoker. We made the base from a thirty-one-gallon aluminum keg that we flipped on its side and turned into a grill and firebox. Above the grill I created a smoker by connecting a dryer vent to a stainless-steel half-barrel beer keg, this one upright, and with a hole cut in the side for a door. We named our creation the "Monstrosity." Almost two decades later, I still use the "Monstrosity" as a grill for videotaped cooking segments or just for backyard fun. For most other smoked and barbecued dishes, I have four or five smokers and grills in different shapes and sizes, including a large offset reverse-flow smoker made from steel pipes. The number of grills I own changes periodically, depending on my needs and what's new on the grill-pit market.

When I'm outdoors preparing étouffée, dirty rice, gumbo, and red beans, I turn to an assortment of cast-iron pots and Dutch ovens, or even to gigantic cast-iron cauldrons. The early Cajuns cooked in cast-iron kettles, and they sure knew what they were doing. You can't beat seasoned cast-iron for naturally keeping food from sticking. Cast-iron also takes the heat from a propane burner or a wood-burning fire. The cast-iron I use the most are several ten- to fifteen-gallon pots. I also have multiple smaller Dutch ovens.

For a big crowd, it's easy to make a large, economical batch of jambalaya, which is typically made with chicken, smoked sausage, and rice. Because of jambalaya's large ratio of rice to meat, a cast-iron pot is a must. Rice sticks to the bottom of anything else and can easily scorch. The thick metal on cast-iron helps with even heat distribution so you can avoid those hot spots. In Louisiana, most decent hardware stores sell the pots and paddles needed to prepare this dish outdoors. I usually cook mine over a propane burner, but if you want to see jambalaya cooked traditionally over an open flame, make a trip to Gonzales, Louisiana, for the annual Jambalaya Festival in May. Contestants are required to prepare their entries over an open fire fueled by "official" Jambalaya Festival wood.

The most popular outdoor pot-cooking in Louisiana is done in the spring, during Louisiana's crawfish season. Industry experts estimate that Louisiana cranks out 90 to 95 percent of the total US production of crawfish, and we eat a whole lot of that total. A huge portion of the catch is boiled in massive aluminum pots. I have several crawfish pots, ranging from one just big enough to cook one thirty-five-pound sack of crawfish to sizes that hold up to three to four sacks at a time.

For roasting whole pigs and other gigantic cuts of meat, I have what we call a "Cajun microwave." Mine is a fairly simple and affordable La Caja China, which is a large wooden box that's lined with thin metal. It rolls on wheels, making it easy to transport. Louisiana has many talented carpenters and welders, and some of them improvise and construct their own Cajun microwaves.

Aside from smokers, grills, pots, and propane burners, I also have a collection of electric knives, food processors, blenders, griddles, and lights. To power up my tools, I use portable generators when necessary. My hoard of cooking equipment is all travel-ready. And it's quite a step up from my humble Weber.

## Let's Get Smoking!

Smokers and grills can cost as little as one hundred dollars or as much as a new car. Before choosing a model, you need to decide if you want something that is strictly for smoking or is dual-purpose, for both smoking and grilling. You also need to think about your level of commitment to tending a fire, and whether you want one that runs on propane, natural gas, electricity, charcoal, or all-wood. All-wood fires give the best smoky flavor, but you have to watch them religiously. Wood and charcoal also burn at a higher level of heat and give a superb sear, but it takes patience to get the blaze where you want it. Sometimes you can't beat propane, gas, and electricity for ease of use.

Smoking requires a covered vessel that maintains a low, steady heat and accommodates some kind of wood for smoke. The main kinds of smokers are water smokers, which are tall vertical metal cylinders or boxes with a water pan above the firebox, which helps give even heat distribution. Horizontal offset smokers give phenomenal smoke flavor through a smoking chamber on the side of the firebox. The hot new thing in smokers is the pellet smoker, which burns compressed wood pellets that are automatically fed to maintain constant temperature.

Grilling is pretty straightforward—just place a metal grill over an open fire, and you're ready to go. A classic mid-level grill is the square or round kettle style on legs. Some have covers and some don't. Depending on your needs, you can buy a lower-level model small enough to carry in a backpack, or you can go all the way up to a luxury built-in stainless body with five burners, porcelain-covered steel grates, and side burners.

Before you think of throwing on an expensive steak or piece of fish, be sure to preheat your grill or smoker. That means starting the fire and leaving it alone until the temperature is right. The next important step is to scrub the grill grates squeaky clean. If you did not scrape everything off after your prior cookout, there's a good chance that harmful bacteria will be thriving on the bits of meat that stayed behind. It's well worth the trouble to get rid of it. Once your grill grates are heated and cleaned, then it's time to oil them.

As for cooking techniques, everyone has their own twists, but the basics remain the same. Proper smoking should be done slowly over low heat and, with the exception of pellet smokers, it definitely requires a true wood fire. Grilling requires that the grill grates first be heated thoroughly and that whatever you're cooking is in the proper place, either over direct or indirect heat. You can expect respectable grill results using all fuel sources. I am, however, a huge fan of live-fire cooking, and I typically use smoldering coals and burning logs to create a high-heat grilling surface. I grew up grilling over open mesquite fires at South Texas hunting camps, and at the family camp in Avoyelles Parish I cooked on a wood-burning stove that mainly burned split pecan and oak. That style of cooking stuck with me, and whenever I get a chance to cook over hardwood flames, I seize it.

At a recent "Glamp-fire" event at Mahaffey Farms outside of Shreveport I cooked a multicourse farm-to-table dinner using nothing but open-fire sources. My staff and I created a mother fire that kept burning all night; then we shoveled hot coals and moved blazing logs from the mother fire to all of our other cooking equipment. I made biscuits in cast-iron Dutch ovens by placing the pots over a bed of coals and adding more red-hot coals on top of the cupped lid. We cooked a whole lamb on a spit above a large firebox, smoking and roast-

A whole lamb cooking on the "Glamp-fire."

**Cooking with open-fire sources.**

ing it at the same time, and we charred carrots over the coals and glazed them with Louisiana cane syrup. The feast made me happy in my soul.

Of course, not all grilling can be done using that kind of fire. Charcoal, wood chunks, and even propane are all there for a reason, and I use them all when I need to or just want to. Charcoal is brilliant for providing that signature grilled flavor. It lights quickly and easily, burns for a reasonably long time, and is easy to keep going for a tailgate party or any extended cook. I enjoy using charcoal for casual backyard grilling and for creating coal beds in large pits, such as an offset smoker.

While some purists absolutely say no to gas or propane grills, when the situation calls for fast and easy heat, I've never been opposed to either. If I'm gearing up for a backyard grilling session for the family or even catering an event that requires a consistently hot grill, I simply heat up the gas grill and use the extra time to savor my beer.

# DEVILED EGGS

MAKES 12

These aren't your grandma's deviled eggs. The Louisiana Molasses Mustard in the ingredient list is a sauce I came up with in 2015, when I was a contestant on *Food Network Star*. This was the first time I ever made this condiment. Celebrity judge Bobby Flay loved it and told me I should bottle it commercially. So guess what? I did!

**1.** Preheat a covered outdoor grill or your oven to 350°F. Separate the egg whites and yolks into two small bowls and set aside. Spray an 8-inch square Pyrex pan with cooking spray and add the unbeaten egg whites to the pan. Cover with foil and place the pan on the grill over indirect heat or into your oven. Cover the grill and cook just until whites are set, about 20 minutes. Remove from grill and let cool, uncovered.

**2.** Whisk yolks until smooth. Coat a nonstick skillet with cooking spray and set it on the medium heat of a propane burner or your stove. Add yolks to the pan and stir until they are set, about 4 to 5 minutes.

**3.** Transfer the cooked yolks to a food processor and add molasses mustard, mayonnaise, olive oil, truffle oil, salt, and pepper. Pulse until smooth and creamy. If mixture gets too thick, add a little more olive oil. Transfer the yolk mixture to a pastry bag with a star piping tip.

**4.** Use a spatula to gently loosen the egg whites in one piece from the pan. Turn the whites over onto a cutting board and cut out 12 pieces with a 2-inch ring mold. Pipe yolks onto whites, and garnish with paprika and green onion, or anything else you desire. Chill until ready to serve.

12 large eggs

Cooking spray

3/4 cup Louisiana Molasses Mustard (purchased or recipe page 184)

2 tablespoons mayonnaise

1 tablespoon olive oil

1 tablespoon truffle oil

1 teaspoon kosher salt

1 teaspoon ground black pepper

Paprika and chopped green onion for garnish

# SPICY AND SWEET BARBECUE POPCORN

MAKES 4 QUARTS

¼ cup canola oil, divided

½ cup popcorn kernels

2 tablespoons Jay D's Spicy & Sweet Barbecue Rub (purchased or recipe page 183, or your favorite commercial brand)

Large pinch of salt

I make giant bowls of this popcorn so that everyone will have something to munch on while appetizers and entrées are grilling. This recipe is easy to make over an outdoor propane burner. The barbecue rub I call for is a commercial product I created to easily give grilled meats such as poultry and pork a perfect seasoning coating. If you can't get your hands on some, mix your favorite Creole seasoning with a little brown sugar, or make the recipe on page 182.

**1.** In a large saucepot or Dutch oven (4 quarts or larger), set the heat of a propane burner or your stove to medium-high. Coat the bottom of the pot with 1 tablespoon canola oil. Add the corn kernels to the pot and top it with the lid. When the kernels start to pop, shake and shuffle the pot over the burner until the popping begins to subside, about 1–2 seconds between pops.

**2.** Remove the pot from heat and pour popped corn into a large bowl. Immediately toss with remaining oil, barbecue rub, and salt. Serve hot.

# LOADED BARBECUE CHEESE FRIES

MAKES 6 SERVINGS

**This dish is always popular with sports crowds, and it's easy to make with frozen fries and bottled ranch dressing. If you want to make your fries from scratch, feel free to start with fresh whole potatoes.**

**1.** Prepare a covered grill for indirect cooking at medium-high heat, or set your oven to 400°F. In a large bowl, toss frozen fries with the olive oil and sprinkle evenly with the barbecue rub. Lay potatoes in a single layer on a foil-lined sheet pan and place over indirect heat in the covered grill or in the oven. Cook until crispy and brown, turning potatoes once. Should take 25–30 minutes.

**2.** While fries are baking, in a small bowl, combine the barbecue sauce and the ranch dressing. Set aside.

**3.** When potatoes are cooked, leave them on the sheet pan and sprinkle with the cheese and jalapeño slices. Put back in the covered grill or in the oven and cook until the cheese is melted. Remove from grill, sprinkle with green onion, and drizzle with the ranch dressing mixture. Serve immediately.

1-pound bag frozen French fries

1 tablespoon olive oil

1 tablespoon Jay D's Spicy & Sweet Barbecue Rub (purchased or recipe page 183, or your favorite commercial brand)

¼ cup Jay D's Louisiana Barbecue Sauce (purchased or recipe page 186, or your favorite commercial brand)

¼ cup bottled ranch dressing

1 cup shredded Monterey Jack cheese

1 fresh jalapeño pepper, sliced

¼ cup sliced green onion

# PIMENTO CHEESE-STUFFED JALAPEÑO PEPPERS

MAKES 24

12 large, fresh jalapeño peppers

¾ cup pimento cheese (recipe follows)

6 strips bacon, cooked and crumbled

**These cheesy, spicy snacks will have your guests reaching for more. And be prepared, they might also crave another beer to wash them down.**

**1.** Preheat a grill to medium-high, or an oven to 375°F. Slice jalapeños lengthwise and remove seeds and membranes. Grill or bake jalapeños, cut side down, for 5 minutes. Let cool.

**2.** Stuff each jalapeño with 1 tablespoon of pimento cheese. Place stuffed peppers, cheese side up, on a sheet of aluminum foil or a sheet pan and grill or bake until cheese is melted, about 10 minutes. Sprinkle with crumbled bacon. Serve warm.

# PIMENTO CHEESE

MAKES ABOUT 3 CUPS

For an extra layer of flavor I use smoked gouda, and to give it another kick I use my Molasses Mustard. Aside from filling jalapeño peppers, I serve pimento cheese with crackers, raw vegetables, on baked potatoes, on burgers, and as a filling for grilled cheese sandwiches.

Combine all ingredients in a bowl and refrigerate at least 30 minutes. Keeps refrigerated up to 3 days.

12 ounces sharp Cheddar cheese, grated

12 ounces smoked Gouda cheese, grated

1 (4-ounce) jar diced pimentos, rinsed

½ cup mayonnaise

2 tablespoons Jay D's Spicy & Sweet Barbecue Rub (purchased or recipe page 183, or your favorite commercial brand)

# GRILLED CHEESE SANDWICHES WITH BARBECUED DATE JAM

MAKES 16 HORS D'OEUVRE SANDWICHES

4 tablespoons Barbecue Compound Butter (recipe page 181)

4 tablespoons Barbecued Date Jam (recipe follows)

8 thick slices country French bread

16 thin slices Brie cheese

Who doesn't love a classic grilled cheese sandwich? How about if we perk it up by slathering on a barbecued date jam.

**1.** Preheat an outdoor grill to medium. Heat a cast-iron grill plate that fits on the grates, or heat a large cast-iron pan. You can also heat the pans on your stove. Add compound butter and cook it until it's golden brown. Meanwhile, spread jam evenly on one side of each slice of bread. Divide Brie among half the bread slices. Top sandwiches with the remaining slices.

**2.** Place as many sandwiches as will fit on the grill plate or in your skillet and cook until golden brown, about 3–5 minutes. Flip and continue cooking until bread is brown and cheese is completely melted. Place grilled sandwiches on a cutting board and use a serrated knife to slice each into 4 pieces. Arrange on a platter and serve immediately.

# BARBECUED DATE JAM

MAKES 1 CUP

5 ounces (a little over 3/4 cup) roughly chopped dried pitted dates

3/4 cup Jay D's Louisiana Barbecue Sauce (purchased or recipe page 186, or your favorite commercial brand)

This easy-to-make spread adds pizzazz to salty sandwich fillings. If you don't have dates, dried figs work well, too.

Add dates and barbecue sauce to a small saucepan and simmer 10 minutes. Puree well in a blender. Keeps a few weeks in the refrigerator.

# DOUBLE SMASHBURGER SLIDERS

**MAKES 8 SLIDERS**

These are called "smashburgers" because you use a firm spatula to smash down hard on sizzling balls of ground beef, which flattens them and gives the meat a crispy outside and juicy interior.

**1.** Use the high heat of a propane burner or your stove to preheat a large flattop griddle or cast-iron pan. Form the ground beef into 16 even-sized balls. Lightly oil the griddle. Mix the sliced onion with a pinch of kosher salt and sauté on the hot flattop, moving the slices of onion around with a spatula until they are soft and brown but not burned. Remove the onions from the griddle and place aside.

**2.** Re-oil the cooking surface. Place the beef balls on the hot griddle, leaving about 3 inches space in between so you have room to flatten them. If your griddle isn't large enough, do it in batches. Right away, use a firm spatula to smash each ball into a round patty slightly larger than the buns. Season the top of each patty with salt and pepper. Cook 2–3 minutes. Scrape the patties from the grill and flip them over. You should see a nice brown crust forming. Sprinkle with salt and pepper and cook another minute or two. Top each patty with a slice of cheese and cook until cheese is melted, about 1 or 2 more minutes.

**3.** Remove the patties from the griddle and layer them on a tray in stacks of two. Using the same griddle, toast the buns 30 seconds to a minute. To build the sliders, place a double beef patty on a toasted bottom bun. Add a nice amount of grilled onions and allow each guest to add their own condiments. Crown the burger with the top bun and dig in.

2 pounds 80/20 ground beef (chuck, brisket, or short rib, nothing lean)

Vegetable oil for brushing the griddle

1 medium white onion, sliced thin

Kosher salt

Ground black pepper

16 slices American cheese

8 slider buns (soft white, brioche, Hawaiian, or potato buns)

For serving: mustard, ketchup, barbecue sauce, mayo, or any condiment you like

# SMOKED TUNA DIP

Wood chips for smoking, soaked in water 30 minutes

2½ pounds yellow fin tuna, cut into ¾-inch steaks

2 cups Jay D's Blanc Du Bois wine, or your favorite dry white wine

2 cups water

¼ cup kosher salt

8 ounces whipped cream cheese

¼ cup Greek yogurt

3 tablespoons Jay D's Louisiana Barbecue Sauce (purchased or recipe page 186, or your favorite commercial brand)

¾ cup diced red onion

1 garlic clove, minced

Zest of one lemon, a few slivers reserved for garnish

½ teaspoon coarsely ground black pepper

¼ cup chopped green onion for garnish

For serving: raw bite-sized vegetables and crackers

**Believe me, this recipe is worth the trouble of setting up your smoker.**

**1.** Set up a smoker with wood chips for indirect heat. Cook the tuna steaks to the side of the heat source to an internal temperature of 250°F.

**2.** In a large bowl or pot, combine the wine, water, and salt. Add the partially cooked tuna steaks and let them brine for an hour in the refrigerator. After brining, pat the tuna steaks dry with paper towels and place them back in the smoker over indirect heat. Cook them through, for about an hour. After tuna is cooked, coarsely chop and allow to cool completely.

**3.** In a mixing bowl, combine whipped cream cheese, yogurt, and barbecue sauce until completely blended. Add the onion, garlic, lemon zest, black pepper, and chopped tuna, and combine completely. Refrigerate at least 20 minutes.

**4.** Garnish your beautiful bowl of dip with chopped green onion and lemon zest. Serve with your favorite fresh vegetables and crackers.

# CRAB DIP

**1.** Gently go through the crab meat with your fingers and pull out all the bits of shell. Set crab aside.

**2.** Preheat a covered grill for indirect heat, or your oven to 350° degrees. In a medium-sized mixing bowl, stir together the cream cheese, mozzarella, sour cream, mayonnaise, hot sauce, lemon juice, garlic powder, paprika, salt, and pepper. Gently fold in the crab meat and the chives.

**3.** Spread the mixture in a small baking pan or casserole dish and cook on the cool side of the covered grill or in your oven until heated through and bubbly, 20–25 minutes. Serve warm with baguette slices or tortilla chips.

1 pound lump crab meat

8 ounces cream cheese, softened

1 cup shredded mozzarella cheese

¼ cup sour cream

¼ cup mayonnaise

1 tablespoon Slap Ya Mama brand hot sauce, or any Louisiana-style hot sauce

1 tablespoon lemon juice

1 teaspoon garlic powder

½ teaspoon paprika

½ teaspoon salt

¼ teaspoon freshly ground black pepper

2 tablespoons chives

For serving: baguette slices or tortilla chips

# CRAWFISH FRITTERS

1 tablespoon butter

1 cup chopped yellow onion, in ¼-inch dice

½ cup chopped bell pepper, in ¼-inch dice

½ cup chopped celery, in ¼-inch dice

1 pound cleaned crawfish tails

2 tablespoons minced garlic

1 cup cornmeal

2 large eggs

1 cup shredded smoked Cheddar cheese

2 cups seasoned seafood breading mix (such as Slap Ya Mama brand Cajun Fish Fry or Louisiana Fish Fry)

Vegetable oil for frying

For serving: 1 cup Barbecue Aioli (recipe page 185)

These are also known as crawfish hushpuppies. Hushpuppies and fritters were some of the main appetizers my fellow cooks and I used to throw into our deep fryers at tailgate parties. We could easily and cheaply feed the masses with fried breads. In 2019, I made a version of this fritter recipe on Food Network's *Beat Bobby Flay,* when I took him down by challenging him to a crawfish boil.

**1.** Heat a skillet over medium-high heat, either over a propane burner or on a stove. Melt butter and add onion, bell pepper, and celery, and sauté until vegetables begin to get soft, about 2–3 minutes. Add crawfish and garlic and sauté an additional 2–3 minutes.

**2.** Place contents of skillet into a mixing bowl. Add cornmeal, eggs, and cheese, and mix well. Use heaping tablespoonfuls to form balls. Roll the balls in breading mix and refrigerate at least 1 hour.

**3.** Heat 2 inches vegetable oil in a deep frying pan or a Dutch oven set over medium-high heat. When oil is hot, drop in the chilled fritters and fry until golden brown, about 3–4 minutes. Drain on paper towels. Serve hot with Barbecue Aioli for dipping.

# GRILLED SHRIMP

MAKES 10 SERVINGS

**These go fast at parties, so you might want to double the recipe.**

**1.** Completely peel and devein the shrimp. Prepare an outdoor or indoor grill for medium heat. In a small bowl, combine the salt, black pepper, paprika, cayenne, and chili powder. On a baking sheet, toss the shrimp with olive oil. Sprinkle the shrimp on both sides with the spice rub.

**2.** Grill the shrimp directly on grill grates until they're pink and slightly charred but not overcooked, 2–3 minutes per side. Throw them into a serving bowl, and put out a box of toothpicks for spearing.

50 large shrimp (21–25 count)

1 tablespoon salt

1 tablespoon ground black pepper

2 teaspoons paprika

1 teaspoon cayenne pepper

1 teaspoon chili powder

¼ cup olive oil

**Crawfish fritters.**

# DUTCH OVEN BISCUITS

MAKES 15 BISCUITS

4 cups all-purpose flour

2 tablespoons baking powder

1½ teaspoons salt

12 tablespoons cold lard or unsalted butter

1½ cups milk or buttermilk

For serving: butter and honey

**This is the kind of biscuit that cooks in wagon trains used to make. I've made them many times on camping trips.**

**1.** Grease the inside of a 4- or 6-quart (10- or 12-inch) cast-iron camp Dutch oven and preheat it to 450°F. (That's 8 coals underneath and 17 coals on top.) In a large bowl, mix together flour, baking powder, and salt. Use a pastry blender, a couple of knives, or your hands to cut in the lard. Work the lard until it is the size of peas. Stir in the milk until the dough looks shaggy.

**2.** Transfer dough to a floured work surface and knead slightly, just until it comes together. Pat dough out ¾ of an inch thick. Use a 2½-inch round cutter to cut biscuits. Pat out scraps and cut more biscuits until all the dough is used.

**3.** Remove the cover from the Dutch oven and arrange the biscuits inside so they're touching but not scrunched. Cover back with the lid and coals (17 on top). Cook biscuits until they're browned and puffed, 10 to 12 minutes.

**4.** Remove the coals from the top, remove the pot from the fire, and uncover. Serve biscuits warm with butter and honey.

# CORNBREAD

MAKES 8 SERVINGS

**1.** Light one side of a covered grill to medium-high, 350–425°F. Place a 9- or 10-inch cast-iron skillet on the grill rack and let it heat 10 minutes. If you're using an oven, place the skillet on a rack and heat the oven to 425°F.

**2.** In a mixing bowl, combine the cornmeal, sugar, baking powder, salt, and soda. Set aside. In another bowl, whisk together the buttermilk, creamed corn, and eggs. Add the dry ingredients to the wet ingredients and whisk until there's no traces of anything dry.

**3.** Carefully remove the skillet from the grill or oven, and coat the inside with the butter. Pour the batter into the hot skillet. The sides of the batter should sizzle and puff up. Place the skillet on the grill rack over indirect heat and cover the grill. Or put it in the oven. Cook until golden brown and the inside springs back when lightly touched, about 25–30 minutes. In the oven, it will take about 20 minutes.

**4.** Flip the hot cornbread onto a cutting board and slice into 8 wedges. Serve warm.

2 cups yellow cornmeal

2 teaspoons sugar

2 teaspoons baking powder

1 teaspoon kosher salt

$\frac{1}{2}$ teaspoon baking soda

1 cup buttermilk, at room temperature

1 cup canned creamed corn

2 large eggs, at room temperature

2 tablespoons melted butter or bacon fat

# PIMENTO CHEESE CORNBREAD

MAKES 8-12 SERVINGS

1½ cups cornmeal

½ cup all-purpose flour

¼ cup sugar

2 teaspoons baking powder

1 teaspoon salt

2 cups buttermilk

2 cups Pimento Cheese
(purchased or recipe page 13)

2 large eggs

2 tablespoons melted butter

**1.** Preheat an outdoor grill or your indoor oven to 350°F. In a medium bowl, combine cornmeal, flour, sugar, baking powder, and salt. Stir in buttermilk, Pimento Cheese, and eggs.

**2.** Swirl the melted butter around the inside of a 9- or 10-inch cast-iron skillet. Pour in the batter and grill over indirect heat, covered, until golden brown and pulling away from the skillet, 35–40 minutes. In the oven, it will take about 30 minutes. Slice into wedges and serve warm.

# KUMQUAT WHISKEY SOUR

MAKES 1 DRINK

In the late fall and throughout the winter, kumquats grow like crazy in south Louisiana. This recipe brings out the best of this sour little citrus fruit, and it's a nice cocktail to sip when you're out tending the grill.

Combine whiskey, lemon juice, and simple syrup in a cocktail shaker. Fill shaker with ice, cover, and shake vigorously 20 seconds. Strain into a rocks glass filled with ice. Garnish with cherry and lemon rind.

2 ounces whiskey

¾ ounce fresh-squeezed lemon juice

¾ ounce Kumquat Simple Syrup (recipe follows)

Ice cubes

For serving: a cherry and a slice of lemon rind

# KUMQUAT SIMPLE SYRUP

MAKES ABOUT 1¾ CUPS

This adds an exciting twist to just about any cocktail that calls for simple syrup.

Combine ingredients in a small saucepan and bring to a boil. Lower heat and simmer, uncovered, 5 minutes. Remove from heat and let sit 10 minutes. Strain into a glass container, while gently pressing the fruit to squeeze out juice. Cover and refrigerate up to 1 week.

1 cup sugar

1 cup water

½ cup kumquats, cut in quarters

**Jay tailgating with the "Monstrosity."**

# TAILGATING

Starting a full twenty-four hours before kickoff, the parking lots surrounding Baton Rouge's Tiger Stadium turn into a sea of purple and gold. Tents pop up on every available inch of space. The air is filled with the sounds of music and televised SEC games, and it's scented with the smell of browning roux, smoldering pecan branches, and wafts of sweet bourbon. On these magical days, when temperatures dip and spirits run high (or are poured into a glass), it's common to find anxious football fans discussing predictions and betting lines. Tailgating cooks, however, focus on barbecuing slabs of pork, stirring cauldrons of jambalaya, frying cracklins, and boiling seafood. Like me, they take their tasks seriously. They're creating these magnificent spreads in less than ideal conditions, and I consider much of what they do a culinary art form.

During my first semester at LSU, my cousin Travis and I took on the duty of cooking for a handful of friends at our tailgate parties. Out on a grassy spot surrounded by a few small trees in front of the LSU Natatorium, we began by grilling simple citrus-marinated chicken, burgers, and sausage. During my second football season, our crowd of friends grew larger and, by year three, hungry Tiger acquaintances were coming in droves. To help feed the hordes, in addition to introducing the aforementioned "Monstrosity" (my barbecue pit made from beer kegs and a welded metal frame), we lugged out huge fryers for fish and hushpuppies. Our updated cooking vessel repertoire also included a cast-iron kettle for making all the one-pot wonders we could dream up.

By that third football season, we were grilling just about any meat and vegetable imaginable. Some of my more successful experiments included grilled okra, mushrooms, zucchini, squash, and eggplant. Sometimes I'd grill watermelon and pineapple for dessert. I also tinkered with upgrading common barbecue dishes, such as using Dr. Pepper to marinate brisket and creating my own spice and herb blends for beer-can chicken.

Time went on and, like a mad chemist, I found myself constantly experimenting with ways to turn the ordinary into something extraordinary. Along the way I also figured out how important it is to cook with the proper seasonings. Back then, there were a few commercial seasoning mixes around, but I wasn't satisfied with any of them, and I was only a novice at mixing my own. My introduction to the commercial world of premixed Cajun spices began in my favorite college course, "Food and Culture in Literature." One of my classmates was Jack Walker, the son of the Ville Platte, Louisiana, family that started the Slap Ya Mama line of seasonings. I loved the flavors that Jack had in that can, and as he and I became friends, we made his outstanding spice mixes, fish-fry (seasoned breading for frying fish), and hot sauce our official tailgating line of seasoning.

By the time I was a senior, my small group of helpers and I had tremendously ramped up the quality of our food. Our menu also expanded, and so did our reputation. We were the talk of the party crowd of Tiger Stadium, and we found ourselves entertaining friends we didn't know we had. Throughout the day, typical attendance at our tailgate parties would be around 300. For a big game, that number could swell up to 500, and there were always around 100 to 150 eating and drinking at any time.

To pay for it all, we'd put out tip jars and sell T-shirts. We took on keg sponsors, and in the spring and summer, we threw off-season fundraising parties like crawfish boils and an annual holiday gala. At that first game, none of us could have imagined the buzz we'd eventually cause. And there's no way that I could have guessed that I was laying the foundation for my eventual career.

## Third Row Tailgaters

For actual football games, I sat with my pals in the student section, in the northwest corner of Tiger Stadium. We always made sure we lined up early to enter. That way we could get our favorite seats, on the third row from the bottom, where we were close to the action and could see the whole field over the heads of the wild fans constantly standing along the railing in front of the first row.

In 2000, with new coach Nick Saban at the helm, unranked LSU hosted ranked Tennessee, a team that also happened to be the defending national champion. In an overtime miracle that occurred right in front of the student section, LSU won the game, launching the stadium into a frenzy. During that game, my friends and I jumped up and down so hard that we broke our aluminum bleacher seat. Right after the game, like most students, I rushed the field. Unbeknownst to me, my cousin Travis and some of his buddies, who were all a couple years older, stayed behind and popped the last remaining

bolt off our bench seat. Another devious soul—we'll call him Scott—took the whole thing and ran with it up the stands, around the concourse, and down the ramps. Then he brought the bench to our tailgate spot and slipped it under my truck.

When I got back to the tailgate party, bright-eyed with purple and gold grass in my hands from the midfield eye of the tiger, I was instructed to take a peak under my truck. To my surprise I observed a five-foot piece of aluminum bleacher. Confused, I ask the gang, "What's that?" They responded that it was literally the third row of Tiger Stadium.

Ever since that day my tailgate friends and I called ourselves the Third Row Tailgaters. With that name in hand, we created a T-shirt logo, a grinning Tiger running off with a piece of a bleacher. We painted that

**Jay with some of the Third Row Tailgaters.**

piece of bench purple, and we all signed it with a gold-paint pen. Our piece of bench became our mascot at tailgate parties, and for years it hung on the wall at my cousin's house. This priceless souvenir from Tiger Stadium currently resides in my house, hanging on my wall.

## Game Day Game Plan

Like most of my friends, real life is pulling me away from grilling in the fields and parking lots surrounding Tiger Stadium. I certainly still go out and root for the Tigers, but after the 2007 National Championship season I hung up my official LSU tailgate chef hat and no longer cooked on campus week in and week out. But during the nearly eight years I was a student, when I cooked at virtually every single home game, I didn't waste a precious second of game day.

LSU's football games usually start around seven p.m., and my buddies and I would drive to campus twelve and a half hours earlier. In my later years, here's what my typical routine looked like:

As soon as I'd arrive on campus I'd have a Bloody Mary, before I had breakfast or did anything. The first order of real business was staking out our usual spot on the front steps of the Natatorium on Nicholson Drive. (For the first half of my tailgating run, that space was grass with a few trees. In the latter years, it was a paved parking lot, but we stayed in the grass next to it.) Our site was close to the oh-so-important public restrooms at the tennis complex, and we

**Overhead view of tailgate at LSU.**

would set up tents, tables, chairs, barbecue pits, propane burners, ice chests, and music.

After setup, it was time to prep some food. We'd rub pork ribs and shoulders with seasoning and stuff duck breasts and jalapeños with cream cheese and wrap them in bacon. Then we'd shuck corn to make maque choux, get roux browning in the cast-iron pot, and the shoulders and rib racks would go in the smoker.

Flying right along, it was on to breakfast, usually Ziploc omelets that were sometimes made with sausage. Plus a side of bacon. Always bacon. And perhaps a shot of bourbon, a ritualistic wakey whiskey.

By midmorning, I'd be stirring gumbo, jambalaya, or red beans. At noon, campus was heating up with fans pouring in. This was the time for basting those pork ribs that had been smoking for hours. When the ribs were finished off, I'd serve them for lunch.

Time for a break. With a cold local brew or a kegged Natty Light in hand, I'd stroll around campus. On these jaunts I found lots of loud music, innumerable ice chests, a wide variety of barbecue pits and smokers, and several kinds of ingenious multiperson beer funnels. When it came to food, it was common to find whole pigs roasting, cracklins frying, jambalaya steaming, and cauldrons of gumbo at a simmer. Probably the most unusual food I've seen cooked on campus was a whole alligator roasting on a rotisserie. Take that, Florida.

If I'd finish my walking beer, a friendly tailgate party would always want to feed me and supply refreshments. You can't beat Tiger hospitality. By the time I'd wander back to home base, it was about three hours before kickoff. More people would have arrived, and I'd throw the stuffed duck breast and jalapeños on the grill, along with some citrus-brined chicken. Around four-thirty, I'd pull off the pork shoulders and serve them as sliders with barbecue sauce. Many of my buddies would eventually mosey over to "Victory Hill" to watch the team, Mike the Tiger, and the band make their way to the stadium. I'd use this opportunity to take a breather.

By five or five-thirty, I'd be finished cooking. That's when fans start heading to the stadium, and we would clean and pack up and follow the crowd to cheer on the Tigers.

Jay relaxing after a day of cooking with the Third Row Tailgaters.

## Tailgating Acclaim

By 2010, I had had plenty of experience with tailgate cooking, so I decided to enter the Comcast Sports South Tony Chachere's Tailgating Cook-Off. This contest was open to all twelve (at the time) SEC universities, and that year I submitted my recipe for Blackberry Bourbon Bone-In Boston Butt, a dish I had been experimenting with for fun. My entry was essentially a pork shoulder that I injected with a mixture of bourbon, blackberry jam, and honey. I rubbed the outside with a mix of Creole seasoning and brown sugar, and smoked it twelve hours over Louisiana pecan.

The contest's elimination process started with online voting that went on during most of the football season. Every week the television show *Comcast SportsNite* featured a different recipe from each of the SEC schools. The top three finalists by online voting would be invited to an actual cook-off in November, which would be held on the LSU campus in Baton Rouge the day of the Ole Miss game. Naturally, I used my newfound blog and social media prowess to urge readers to vote for me. This was when I learned the true power of social media. This contest gave me experience in something else important—I appeared on a local news show to promote my entry, and I did a live television cooking demo, something I'd never before done.

**Jay at Tony Chachere's Tailgating Cook-Off at LSU.**

After months of campaigning, my recipe claimed the top SEC spot, with 75,357 votes. The contestant from Ole Miss, Jack Koban, who is now a friend, came in second with 67,475. The cook-off between the two of us, plus a third finalist from Mississippi State, took place on November 20 in the hours before LSU played Ole Miss. By daybreak, I had unloaded the "Monstrosity" and was set up and pumped up, ready to show my stuff to an overflow of football fans. I lit up my smoker. I faced the camera. And I kicked (pardon the pun) butt. My Blackberry Bourbon Boston Butt won first place!

I still use my prizes, which were an assortment of cooking gadgets and Tony Chachere logo items, and a Big Green Egg charcoal grill and smoker that I turn to constantly. These gifts will always remind me of my first major cooking contest win, and also of the first time I cooked for a television audience. I'll always be thankful for that contest. Who knows where I'd be if I hadn't been crowned king of SEC tailgate cooking.

### Tailgating Stardom

I'm sure you've heard of Fox TV's *MasterChef,* the reality show open to amateur and home chefs. Immediately, as in minutes, after I won the Tony Chachere's Tailgating Cook-Off, I attached my still-smoking barbecue pit to the back bumper of my truck. But instead of walking to the football game, I drove eighty miles from Baton Rouge to New Orleans and went to a casting call for *MasterChef.*

Several months earlier, I had submitted an online application for season two of *MasterChef.* At the time, I'd never done any TV, but the program's casting producers checked out my blog and online tailgating videos and told me not to miss that casting call in New Orleans. For that contest's signature dish, out of the smoker I pulled a Blackberry Bourbon Boston Butt I'd already cooked. A month later, I was named one of the top hundred amateur chefs in America. This certainly was an honor, but it also meant I'd be cooking against ninety-nine equally talented peers. Just as intimidating, I'd be judged by celebrity chef Gordon Ramsay, winemaker and restaurateur Joe Bastianich, and chef Graham Elliot.

We taped the show in February 2011 and were competing for the coveted white apron and the chance to advance to the next round of competition. I had one hour to prepare a signature dish. I chose an herb-roasted rack of venison with a Cajun shrimp and cornbread-stuffed bell pepper. I thought it was a winner. Unfortunately, the judges didn't agree, and I went home.

By now, however, I was seriously infected with the culinary bug. From then on, I spent a lot of my time laying the groundwork for success, mainly by honing my cooking skills, hosting my radio show, researching and writing about food and beverages, and getting way more experience in front of television cameras. Then in 2013, the unimaginable happened: I was chosen for a big-time casting call for season ten of the Food Network's *Food Network Star,* one of television's biggest cooking competition shows. Eclipsing my wildest dreams, I got several callbacks. But unfortunately, I was eventually edged out of the cast.

The following year the Food Network wasn't casting for *Food Network Star* in New Orleans. And I wasn't going to try out by driving seven and a half hours to Dallas, the closest city with open casting calls, especially after I'd made it so far the previous year. Fortunately, the producers remembered me, and I received a phone call asking if I'd be interested in doing the show's season eleven. I said, "Of course!" After a few Skype interviews with the producers, I earned a coveted spot.

In February and March of 2015, we filmed the show in Los Angeles. With Bobby Flay, Giada DeLaurentiis, and rotating guest judges watching intently, I cooked Louisiana tailgating food against eleven outstanding chefs. Every week of the eleven episodes, I got better and better, and I went all the way to the final three. My hopes were stratospheric. Then I learned on the finale that I came in runner-up. I don't think I've ever been so disappointed.

Sure, losing was a letdown, but lots of great things happened because of that show. For example, a few weeks after the competition was aired, I got another call from the Food Network. While competing on the *Food Network Star* finale, I hosted a pilot called *Deep Fried America,* while being mentored by cooking personality Rachael Ray. The network asked if I was still interested in pursuing the show. Once again, "Of course!" So I slipped away to Austin, Texas, and worked with Magnetic Productions to film a half-hour episode. In the summer of 2016 that pilot aired on the Travel Channel.

Unfortunately, the Travel Channel didn't pick up my show. But no matter what happens in the future, I'll be eternally grateful to the Food Network for giving me that initial national presence on *Food Network Star*. I performed better than I could have ever imagined, having never been up for

**Jay posing with some legends in Austin, Texas.**

On August 4, 2017, Jay delivered the keynote address at LSU's 293rd commencement. Afterwards, Jay treated the graduates to barbecue inside Tiger Stadium.

elimination during the entire eleven-week broadcast. I did have a few screw-ups, though, especially during the third week. That's when I botched a chicken-and-okra gumbo. For that segment, I had to create a slimy soup, so naturally I based a gumbo around okra. Had I thought it through, I would have realized I didn't have enough time to make a respectable gumbo. I also didn't have smoked sausage. I had to use scraps of chicken from a picked over carcass, and I had to use store-bought stock. My roux wasn't dark enough, and I made too much of it for the gumbo, making it way too thick. But I was a smashing success at making my gumbo slimy. My okra-laced gumbo had to sit in a refrigerator for three hours before judging, and by then, it was gelatinous mess. When I served this so-called gumbo to the judges, the flavor was there, but it wasn't a proper gumbo.

I am, however, also remembered for my biggest *Food Network Star* success. During the episode that ran the week after the Fourth of July we had to use the other team's groceries. I lucked up and got to take another stab at cooking okra, this time as a side dish alongside prime rib eyes. I stewed the okra perfectly with tomatoes and garlic, and I put beautiful sears on the steaks and served them medium rare. I was killing it, and I almost felt like I was cheating.

I think one of the reasons I got as far as I did on that show was because of my experience on the radio; performing in front of that camera felt so natural. Bob Tuschman, vice president for Food Network and a judge, declared I was the "the most camera-ready contestant we've ever had on *Food Network Star.*" Another big advantage was my love and knowledge of cooking tailgate food. There's no way I could have seriously competed on a first-rate reality show without the lessons I learned while grilling for the hungry crowds at LSU.

# BREAKFAST SCRAMBLE

MAKES 6 SERVINGS

1. In a large bowl, whisk eggs well, until all streaks of the whites disappear. Whisk in salt and pepper. Set aside.

2. In a very large skillet set over the medium heat of a propane burner or your kitchen stove, add olive oil and sauté sausage, tomatoes, and leek until leek is wilted and the sausage is browned.

3. Add the eggs and scramble them with a spatula until they are no longer runny, but aren't completely dried out. Garnish with chopped peanuts and sliced green onion. Serve hot.

9 large, fresh eggs

Kosher salt and freshly ground black pepper to taste

1 tablespoon extra virgin olive oil

1/2 pound smoked pork sausage, cut into 1/2-inch cubes

2 medium Creole tomatoes, seeded and chopped

1 medium leek, white and light-green parts only, cut crosswise into 1/4-inch rounds

For serving: cilantro and 6 radishes shaved thin on a mandoline slicer

# SHRIMP AND PINEAPPLE SKEWERS

MAKES 4 SERVINGS

1. Soak skewers in water 20 minutes. Preheat an outdoor or indoor grill to 375°F. Whisk together vinegar, soy sauce, and honey. Set aside.

2. Alternately thread shrimp, pineapple, mushrooms, and onion onto skewers. Brush everything with canola oil, and sprinkle with salt and pepper.

3. Place skewers on the hot grill. Cook until shrimp begin to turn opaque, about 2 minutes. Brush with the soy sauce mixture. Flip each skewer and brush with sauce again. Grill until shrimp turn completely opaque and vegetables are lightly charred, 2 to 3 more minutes. Remove from grill and serve warm.

12 (8- to 10-inch) wooden skewers

3 tablespoons rice vinegar

2 tablespoons low-sodium soy sauce

2 tablespoons local honey

1 pound large shrimp, peeled, deveined, tail on

1/2 of a fresh pineapple, peeled, cored, and cut into 1/2-inch cubes

1 pound fresh mushrooms, halved

1 red onion, cut into 1/2-inch pieces

2 tablespoons canola oil

Salt and ground black pepper

# LOUISIANA CEVICHE

MAKES 12 APPETIZER SERVINGS

1 pound red snapper fillet, cut in 3/4–inch pieces (or substitute any fresh white, flaky fish)

1/2 pound extra-large cooked shrimp, cut into 1-inch pieces

1/2 pound fresh lump crab meat, picked over for shells

2 cups minced green bell pepper

2 cups minced red onion

3 avocados, halved, pitted, peeled, and chopped

1 (16-ounce) container grape tomatoes, halved

1 1/2 cups fresh lime juice, plus additional if needed

1 cup fresh lemon juice, plus additional if needed

1/4 cup pineapple juice

1/2 cup chopped cilantro

1/2 cup chopped parsley

2 1/2 teaspoons kosher salt

1 teaspoon ground black pepper

For serving: crackers or tortilla chips

**Red snapper is one of the many exquisite fish we catch in the Gulf of Mexico. If you don't have access to red snapper, you can substitute any flaky white fish. Served in a deep platter, this dish makes a striking display.**

**1.** In a large nonreactive bowl (stainless steel, enamel-coated, or glass), combine all ingredients until uniformly mixed. Make sure fish, shrimp, and crab are submerged. If not, add more lime or lemon juice.

**2.** Cover the bowl so that it is airtight and refrigerate a minimum of 12 hours. Taste and add more salt and pepper if necessary. Serve chilled with crackers or tortilla chips.

# CAJUN CRAWFISH BREAD

MAKES 8 SERVINGS

**This hot, melty, crunchy bread is perfect for serving at football parties. If you cook it on a charcoal grill, the bread picks up a subtle smoky flavor.**

**1.** Preheat a grill or your oven to 375°F. Cut bread in half lengthwise. Place cut sides up on a foil-lined cookie sheet and spread with mayonnaise. Set aside.

**2.** In a large, heavy-bottomed skillet set over medium heat of a propane burner or your stove, melt the butter and sauté the yellow onion until it is soft, about 5 minutes. Add the garlic and continue to sauté until fragrant, about 2 minutes. Add the crawfish, green onion, and parsley. Stir and cook 5 minutes. To the sautéed mixture, stir in the cream cheese and Cajun seasoning.

**3.** Spread mixture evenly over each half of the sliced French bread. Top with Parmesan cheese, then Pepper Jack cheese and paprika. Place the open-faced sandwiches on the cookie sheet on the grill, close the cover, and cook until heated through thoroughly, about 15 minutes. Will take the same amount of time in your indoor oven. If you're cooking in your kitchen, turn on the broiler and broil about 2 minutes. Top with fresh parsley. Slice into portions and serve warm.

1 (15-inch) loaf French bread

½ cup mayonnaise

2 tablespoons butter

¾ cup diced yellow onion

3 cloves fresh garlic, minced

1 pound Louisiana crawfish tails, with fat

¾ cup chopped green onion

1 tablespoon chopped fresh parsley, plus more for garnish

1 (8-ounce) package cream cheese, softened to room temperature

1 teaspoon Cajun seasoning (purchased or recipe page 182)

½ cup grated Parmesan cheese

¾ cup shredded Pepper Jack cheese

½ teaspoon paprika

# CRAWFISH ÉTOUFFÉE ARANCINI

MAKES 24 APPETIZER-SIZED FRIED BALLS

1 recipe Crawfish Étouffée, without the rice (recipe page 106)

8 cups water

4 cups raw long-grain rice

Vegetable oil for frying

12 large eggs

Panko breadcrumbs for coating

Kosher salt for sprinkling

**This is basically crawfish jambalaya formed into balls and fried. You can make the base mixture a day ahead. I take chilled, unfried arancini base to parties and fry it up at the venue so it's nice and hot. These crispy crawfish balls are a great crowd pleaser.**

1. Make the recipe for Crawfish Étouffée and set aside.

2. Over the medium-high heat of a propane burner or your stove, bring the water to a boil and lower to a simmer. Add the rice and stir. Cover the pot and simmer until the rice has absorbed all the water and is tender, about 20 minutes.

3. After rice is cooked, stir it into the crawfish étouffée and transfer the mixture to a large sheet pan or mixing bowl that fits in the refrigerator. Refrigerate until completely cooled. (Can be made a day ahead to this point.)

4. When you're ready to serve, in a heavy bottomed pot or Dutch oven heat 2 inches vegetable oil to 350°F. Form the rice-and-crawfish mixture into ping-pong-sized balls. Place the eggs in a large bowl and beat them well. Place the breadcrumbs in another bowl. One at a time, dip the balls into the beaten eggs, then coat with panko breadcrumbs. Immediately drop them into the hot oil. Fry each ball until golden brown, 4–5 minutes. Sprinkle with kosher salt and serve hot.

# CHICKEN AND ANDOUILLE GUMBO

MAKES 8–10 SERVINGS

**Gumbo was always a favorite at my tailgate parties. I make mine the Cajun way, with a lot of dark roux. And I don't use tomato, an ingredient that's traditional in Creole-style gumbo.**

**1.** Place the water in a large stockpot. Add the chicken, quartered onion, carrots, stalks of celery, peppercorns, and bay leaves. Bring to a boil over a propane burner or your stove and cook 1 hour. Strain, reserving chicken and stock. Debone the chicken, removing as much of the skin and bones as possible. Discard skin and bones and shred the meat. Set aside.

**2.** To make a roux, heat bacon fat in a 2-gallon stockpot or a Dutch oven over the medium-high heat of a propane burner or stove. Whisk in flour and stir constantly until the mixture turns dark brown. Do not let it scorch. If black specks appear, discard and begin again.

**3.** Add diced onion, diced celery, and bell pepper. Sauté until vegetables are wilted, about 5 minutes. Add the andouille and garlic and sauté until andouille is brown, another 10 minutes. Blend in the shredded chicken and sauté 5 minutes.

**4.** One ladle at a time, add reserved chicken stock, stirring constantly until all is incorporated. Bring to a rolling boil, reduce to a simmer, and cook 1 hour. Skim any fat that rises to the top.

**5.** Add 1 cup of green onion, thyme, oregano, and bay leaf. Add the Cajun seasoning and continue to simmer 30 minutes. Season to taste using salt, pepper, and hot sauce. Add parsley and simmer another 5 minutes. Serve hot in bowls over white rice, using the remaining green onion for garnish.

1 gallon water

1 whole chicken

1 medium onion, peeled and quartered, plus 2 cups diced

2 carrots, peeled

2 stalks celery, plus 2 cups diced

2 tablespoons whole black peppercorns

2 bay leaves

1 cup bacon fat, or 1/2 cup each canola oil and butter

1 1/2 cups all-purpose flour

1 cup diced bell pepper

1 pound andouille sausage, cut into half or quarter moons

1/4 cup minced garlic

2 cups sliced green onion, divided

2 sprigs thyme

2 teaspoons dried oregano

1 bay leaf

2 teaspoons Cajun seasoning (purchased or recipe page 182)

Salt and cracked black pepper to taste

Louisiana hot sauce to taste

1/2 cup chopped parsley

4 cups cooked white rice (recipe page 166)

# CAJUN CHICKEN AND SMOKED SAUSAGE JAMBALAYA

MAKES 8-10 SERVINGS

2 tablespoons canola oil

2 cups sliced smoked sausage

2 cups diced dark-meat chicken

1 cup diced pork shoulder

2 cups diced yellow onion

1 cup diced green bell pepper

1 cup diced celery

¼ cup minced garlic

1 tablespoon Cajun seasoning
(purchased or recipe page 182)

5 cups chicken broth

Salt and pepper to taste

3 cups raw Louisiana long-grain rice

½ cup sliced green onion

½ cup minced parsley

**New Orleans is known for its Creole-style jambalaya, which is made with tomato, and the finished dish is red. Cajun jambalaya doesn't have tomato, and it turns out brown. I usually cook Cajun jambalaya, which is the kind my Maw Maw and my mom always made.**

**1.** In a large cast-iron pot, heat oil over a medium-high flame on a propane burner or your stove. Add sausage, chicken, and pork shoulder and brown well, about 12 minutes. Remove meats and let dry on paper towels. Leave any rendered fat in the pot.

**2.** To the same pot, add onion, bell pepper, and celery. Sauté until soft, about 6 minutes. Add garlic and sauté 1 minute. Add meats back to pot and stir in Cajun seasoning, then chicken broth. Simmer 30 minutes, covered.

**3.** Taste the liquid for seasoning; it should be slightly salty and well-flavored. If not, add salt and pepper. With pot at a boil, stir in rice. When it comes back to a second boil, stir it, cover with a lid, and lower heat to a simmer. Cook until liquid is completely absorbed and rice is tender, 20–30 minutes.

**4.** Remove pot from the heat and let it sit 5 minutes. Remove the pot cover and toss in green onion and parsley. Fold rice over from the bottom of the pot to the top. To avoid overcooking the rice, cool slightly with the lid off. Serve jambalaya warm.

# BEER-CAN CHICKEN

4 SERVINGS

**1.** Preheat one side of a grill with a tall cover to 350°F. Pat chicken dry and brush with canola oil. Sprinkle chicken with salt, then massage with Cajun seasoning.

**2.** Empty out (or drink!) $1/4$ of the can of beer. Carefully ease the chicken's cavity down (legs down) over the beer can until it's in as far as it can go. Stand chicken up on the cool side of the grill and cover. After 45 minutes, turn chicken around halfway. Cook until chicken reaches 170–180°F in the meatiest part of the thighs, about $1^{1}/_{2}$–2 hours total.

**3.** Remove chicken from grill and let rest for 15 minutes before serving. Be careful when removing the beer can; the beer will be hot.

1 (3- to 4-pound) whole chicken

1 tablespoon canola oil

2 teaspoons kosher salt

3 tablespoons Cajun seasoning (purchased or recipe page 182)

1 (12-ounce) can beer

# BLACKBERRY BOURBON BONE-IN BOSTON BUTT

MAKES 20 SERVINGS

1 large (8- to 10-pound) bone-in Boston butt pork shoulder

1 cup bourbon

1 cup blackberry jam

⅓ pound of local honey (⅜ cup)

2 tablespoons freshly ground black pepper

A food injector for liquid seasoning

2 cups Jay D's Spicy & Sweet Barbecue Rub (purchased or recipe page 183, or your favorite commercial brand)

Louisiana pecan wood chips, soaked in water 30 minutes

For serving: buns, optional

**This is the recipe I concocted to win the Tony Chachere's Tailgate Cook-Off Award, which pretty much launched my career in the food media business.**

**1.** Trim excess fat from pork shoulder. In a small mixing bowl or a food processor, blend together the bourbon, blackberry jam, honey, and black pepper. Use the food injector to inject the mixture into the pork shoulder on all sides, getting it around the bone and throughout the meat.

Rub the outside of the pork shoulder with barbecue rub, making sure to coat all sides liberally.

**2.** Prepare a smoker with the pecan wood and heat it to 225°F. Smoke the pork shoulder until it's fall-apart tender, about 12 hours. You can also roast it in a 275°F oven for 6 to 8 hours, depending on size.

**3.** Allow the pork to cool until it is comfortable enough to handle. Using a couple of forks or your hands, shred the pork apart. Eat it on its own or serve on buns as pulled-pork sandwiches.

# SKIRT STEAK FAJITAS

MAKES 6–8 SERVINGS

**1.** Preheat a grill to 375°F. In a medium bowl, whisk together marinade ingredients. Set aside enough marinade to toss with the vegetables, about ¼ cup. Put the skirt steak in a large food-safe plastic bag and add remaining marinade. Seal and shake the bag to make sure the meat is well coated. Refrigerate 8 hours or overnight.

**2.** A few hours before grilling time, toss the peppers and onion in a bowl with the reserved ¼ cup marinade. Remove the steak from the marinade. Let the excess marinade drip off and transfer the steak to a large plate. Let it come to room temperature.

**3.** When ready to cook, preheat a grill to 375°F. Put a large cast-iron skillet on one side of the grill and add the onions and peppers and their marinade. Place the skirt steak on the other side of the grill. Cover the grill and cook, turning the steak occasionally, until nicely seared and medium-rare (about 130–135°F). Stir the vegetables every once in a while.

**4.** Thinly slice the steak against the grain. Slide the slices into the frying pan with the peppers and onions, which by now should be completely tender. Serve the meat and vegetables wrapped in warm tortillas and topped with pico de gallo, sour cream, guacamole, and cheese.

1½ pounds skirt steak

1 red bell pepper, stemmed, seeded, and cut into strips

1 green bell pepper, stemmed, seeded, and cut into strips

1 large yellow onion, halved and sliced

For serving: 16 warm, fresh tortillas (purchased or recipe page 175), pico de gallo, sour cream, guacamole, and shredded Jack cheese

Marinade:

⅓ cup soy sauce

⅓ cup orange juice

⅓ cup lime juice

⅓ cup canola oil

¼ cup chopped fresh cilantro

Zest of 1 orange

5 cloves garlic, minced

2 tablespoons brown sugar

2 teaspoons chili powder

2 teaspoons ground cumin

# LAMB MEATBALLS

MAKES 24 SMALL MEATBALLS

1 pound ground lamb

1½ cups finely chopped fresh mint, loosely packed

3 tablespoons finely chopped red onion

3 garlic cloves, minced

1 egg, beaten

2 tablespoons bread crumbs

1 tablespoon mayonnaise

1 teaspoon cumin

¾ teaspoon kosher salt

**1.** Preheat a covered grill or your oven to 375°F. Add all ingredients to a large bowl and use your hands to mix evenly. Use a teaspoon to form the mixture into 24 meatballs. (Don't level the meat off or pack the meatballs too tightly.)

**2.** Place meatballs on a greased sheet pan and cover with foil. Place sheet pan in the covered grill, or in your oven. Cook fully, to a 160°F internal temperature. Should take 15–20 minutes. Serve warm.

# STRAWBERRY-BASIL BOURBON SMASH

MAKES 6-8 DRINKS

5 ounces fresh basil leaves, about 3½ cups chopped and loosely packed

2 cups strawberries, stemmed

2 cups sugar

2 cups water

2 cups bourbon

Ice

**This is a good drink for casual outdoor entertaining in the summer, when basil grows like crazy in south Louisiana.**

**1.** Add basil, strawberries, sugar, and water to a large saucepan. Cook over medium heat until the sugar dissolves and the liquid reduces by half. Pour into a blender and puree until smooth. Refrigerate in a large pitcher until well chilled.

**2.** Stir the bourbon into the puree in the pitcher. Pour into ice-filled rocks glasses and serve.

# LOUISIANA BLOODY MARY

MAKES 1 TALL DRINK

I call this a Louisiana Bloody Mary because all the ingredients
are made in our state. Oryza vodka, by the way, is one of only two
American vodkas distilled with rice.

Dip the rim of a tall drink glass into water and then into the barbecue rub.
Fill a cocktail shaker with ice and add Bloody Mary mix, vodka, and barbecue
sauce. Shake well for 15 seconds. Pour into the prepared glass. Garnish and
serve.

Jay D's Spicy & Sweet Barbecue
Rub (purchased or recipe page 183,
or your favorite commercial brand)

Ice

6 ounces Louisiana-made Bloody
Mary Mix (I use Louisiana Sisters
brand)

2 ounces Oryza Vodka

2 tablespoons Jay D's Louisiana
Barbecue Sauce (purchased or
recipe page 186, or your favorite
commercial brand)

For serving: pickled okra, spicy
green beans, and a boiled crawfish
or shrimp if you like

# STARGAZER COCKTAIL

MAKES 1 DRINK

Muddle the pineapple in a cocktail shaker. Fill the shaker with ice. Add wine,
rum, and simple syrup. Shake vigorously and strain into whatever cup you
have on hand. If you want to get fancy, use a chilled Collins glass. To garnish,
spear the lime wedge and pineapple chunk with a toothpick and lay on top of
the cup rim. Serve immediately.

1 tablespoon grilled pineapple
(recipe follows)

Ice

2 ounces Jay D's Blanc du Bois wine,
or your favorite dry white wine

1 ounce dark rum

1/2 ounce vanilla bean simple syrup

For serving: lime wedge and a
grilled pineapple chunk

# GRILLED PINEAPPLE

MAKES 4 SERVINGS

1 fresh pineapple

Coconut oil

**Grilled pineapple is a natural alongside pork, or chop it up and stir it into your favorite store-bought salsa.**

Peel and core the pineapple and cut it horizontally into 1-inch slices. Preheat an outdoor or indoor grill to medium-high, 375–400°F. Brush pineapple with coconut oil and grill over direct heat until lightly charred on both sides, about 3 minutes per side. Serve warm or at room temperature.

# LOUISIANA RUM PUNCH

MAKES 8 CUPS

2 cups ginger ale

2 cups orange juice

2 cups pineapple juice

1 cup silver or clear rum

1 cup spiced rum

Ice

For serving: orange slices and pineapple chunks

**This recipe tastes best if everything is chilled before mixing.**

Combine punch ingredients in a gallon-sized container. Fill container with ice. Pour punch into cups and decorate rims with orange slices and chunks of pineapple.

# PORK

When I'm smoking and grilling for a crowd, my go-to meat is often pork, which is one of the best bargains around. And who can turn down an insanely moist, tender pulled-pork sandwich or a perfectly smoked and saucy rack of ribs?

Aside from low supermarket prices, pork is popular here because pigs reproduce rapidly, they're extremely easy to raise, and they've been around for a long time. In the 1500s, Spanish explorers brought pigs to the American South. Some of those pigs became feral and ran around wild. In Louisiana's early days, farmers also let most of their domestic pigs roam free. A family might have kept a few penned up and fed those pampered animals table scraps. The majority of the sounder (the correct word for a herd), however, fended for themselves in pastures and swamps, and were rounded up when it was time for slaughter. Laws eventually prohibited owners from letting their porkies wander at will, but until then, it was every free-roaming pig for itself.

Today, penned-up pigs still often serve as family garbage disposals, and they're also supplemented with commercial feeds. The last couple of decades have also seen the rise of large industrial farms, where pigs are mostly fed bulk grain feeds, and which accounts for the abundance of pork at the grocery store.

As far as flavor goes, one of the darkest times for good-tasting pork was the era in which I grew up, the 1990s, when pork fat was considered the enemy. Most consumers back then believed that lard and highly marbled cuts of pork were less healthful than artificial trans fats, which we have recently learned is our health's real villain. But before we picked up on that valuable research, large pork breeders responded to the fat scare by raising lean pigs, which led to tasteless pork in grocery stores.

The no-pork-fat trend, I am happy to report, is changing. In south Louisiana, it's now even possible to purchase the more marbled and tasty Berkshire and Mandalista breeds. I buy a lot of my pork from Iverstine Family Farms, which is in St. Helena Parish, north of Baton Rouge. Iverstine raises heritage breed Berkshires in wooded lots, which allows them to eat naturally falling

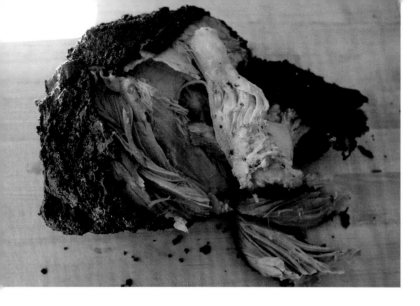

**Jay D's triple-threat pork shoulder.**

acorns. These lucky pigs also wallow and roam freely. Small specialized farms such as Iverstine, as well as Mahaffey Farms outside of Shreveport, are popping up all over, which makes it easier for consumers to find chops and roasts that taste like real pork.

## Celebrating Every Squeal

Pork is an important staple in Louisiana, and we've grown famous for our outstanding ways of cooking and preserving every single piece of a pig, including the less desirable parts. Much of pork offal is transformed into finger foods that are easily found in meat markets, but they're also sold in barrooms and convenience stores. On the counters of these places you can find rice steamers filled with hot white boudin (ground offal and rice stuffed into intestine), and if you're lucky you'll stumble upon someone who sells boudin noir (pork and pig blood boudin). You'll also find gallon jars filled with pickled pig snouts and feet. Cracklins (fried pork belly) are sold by the pound, as is hog's head cheese (traditionally, meat from the hog's head molded in a gelatin made from ground pig's foot and head cartilage). Chitlins, a pig's sterilized small intestine, is common in the meat sections of grocery stores, as are chaurice, a local breakfast sausage, and pickle meat, strips of spicy preserved pork butt used for seasoning.

Before refrigeration, when it was essential for Louisiana's country families to gather and butcher their own pigs, usually around November at an event called a boucherie, most of what wasn't immediately consumed ended up in the smokehouse. Cajuns are masters at smoking pork, and until not too long ago virtually every farm house in Acadiana had its own smokehouse.

Today, smoking is mostly used for flavoring, and most Cajuns buy smoked meats from grocery stores and specialty meat shops, where it's easy to find tasso, andouille, ham hocks, bacon, and an eye-popping selection of smoked sausage. My father's family comes from Cottonport, a small town in Avoyelles Parish, in the northern part of Acadiana, in a region where smoked pork is especially appreciated for its flavoring power. Whether it's beans, gumbo, potatoes, or meat stuffings, one of the main ingredients is likely to be some cut of Cajun-style meat that's heavily peppered and smoked to the color of deep mahogany.

In Cottonport, the best place to buy smoked specialties is at T-Jim's Grocery, a cinderblock establishment that sells some of the tastiest boudin (including boudin noir), smoked sausage, and hogshead cheese around. The busiest smoked-meat markets are in Scott and near Lafayette, the "capital" of Acadiana, and in Ville Platte, the self-proclaimed "Smoked Meat Capital of the World." I regularly visit as many Cajun meat markets as I can.

To honor our love of pork, Louisiana holds a near endless amount of pork-themed festivals. Scott, Louisiana, has the Boudin Festival. Ville Platte has the annual Smoked Meat Festival, and there's the Andouille Festival in LaPlace, the Swine Festival in Basile, the Cracklin Festival in Port Barre, and the Cochon de Lait festival in Mansura, a small town in Avoyelles Parish, which is close to the middle of the state.

There's also outstanding barbecued pork and cochon de lait at one of Louisiana's biggest outdoor cooking contests, Hogs for the Cause. This barbecue cook-off is in New Orleans, and it raises money for children with pediatric brain cancer. In 2013, Galen Iverstine of Iverstine Farms and I created a team we named "Bacon Rouge." That first year we entered against over seventy teams, which were mostly from New Orleans, and we took sixth place in the "porkpourri" category, for Chocolate Covered Bacon with Crumbled Pork Rinds. The next year our team grew, and we took eighth place for our ribs and fourth place in the Camelia Brand Red Bean category, with our entry of Red Bean and Rice Balls with Barbecue Aioli. In 2015, the one year it seems it didn't rain, we won first place in the pork shoulder (butt) category. In 2016, against

Hogs for the Cause 2015.

some ninety teams, we took eleventh place in ribs and second in the Blue Plate brand side-item category with our Barbecue Elote, a take on the popular Mexican corn-on-the cob street food.

Lately, my hectic schedule hasn't allowed me to enter Hogs for the Cause or any other statewide pork-cooking contest. But like most people in Louisiana, I take eating and cooking pork seriously, and I hope that soon I can find the time to compete again.

## The Cochon de Lait

To feed a large crowd, I often cook a whole pig the Cajun way, by preparing a cochon de lait. Literally meaning "pig in milk," the process starts with a cleaned suckling pig that is partially split along its backbone, spread flat, and rubbed or injected with a potent blend of spices. The old way of cooking cochon de lait is to sandwich the pig between two sheets of reinforcing wire and tie it securely. The makeshift roasting rack is hung from a wooden or metal crossbar, such as an old swing set, and suspended over a two-foot-deep firepit of slow-burning coals. A more modern method is to construct a six-by-six-by-six-foot "cooking shed" made of tin and mount an electric rotisserie onto the shed's ceiling. The pig hangs from the rotisserie and slowly turns over a fire. When I roast a whole pig, I typically use my La Caja China, the portable "Cajun microwave" described in chapter 1. Since this versatile oven cooks food below a charcoal or wood fire, I easily get the flavor and texture I want.

A whole pig is done when the skin turns deep bronze and crisp, and the flesh underneath falls apart. With a La Caja China, this takes about four to five hours, depending on the size of the pig. Some of the other methods can take up to twelve hours, or a whole night. During the idle hours of tending any cochon de lait fire, music is played and stories are told, and I can personally attest that many cans of beer and fifths of bourbon are consumed. But that's the way of south Louisiana; when your family and a bunch of friends gather to partake of something as extraordinary as a whole roasted pig, you have to break out a toast.

# CRACKLINS

**Cracklins are extremely common in southwest Louisiana, where assorted mom-and-pop stores informally vie for the title of best cracklin maker.**

5 pounds pork belly

1 quart lard

Peanut oil for frying

Cracklin Seasoning (recipe follows)

**1.** Skin side up, cut pork belly into 1-inch cubes. In a large Dutch oven, spoon in lard, then lay in the pork belly pieces in no more than 3 layers. Set a propane burner or your stove to medium-high heat and bring the pork to a boil, stirring frequently to avoid sticking. Reduce heat to medium and cook until skins blister and turn golden brown. This can take 50–55 minutes.

**2.** Transfer fried pork belly pieces to baking sheets and refrigerate until cold. Strain lard and reserve for another use.

**3.** In a large Dutch oven, pour 4 inches of peanut oil and heat until a thermometer reads 380°F. Fry chilled cracklins in batches until golden brown and puffy, and you hear them "pop." This should only take 5–6 minutes. Let cracklins drain on a sheet pan lined with paper towels. Liberally sprinkle hot cracklins with Cracklin Seasoning. Serve hot. You can also eat them at room temperature, but they're not as tasty.

# CRACKLIN SEASONING

MAKES ABOUT 1¾ CUPS

**Try rubbing leftover crackling seasoning on fat pork chops.**

¾ cup chili powder

¾ cup fine salt

¼ cup ground black pepper

¼ cup garlic powder

¼ cup onion powder

¼ cup celery salt

¼ cup sugar

2 teaspoons cayenne pepper

Combine everything together and store in an airtight container.

# FRESH BREAKFAST SAUSAGE

MAKES 8 PATTIES

1 pound ground pork butt, with a lot of the fat

2 teaspoons honey

1 garlic clove, finely minced

1 teaspoon kosher salt

1 teaspoon finely chopped fresh sage leaves

1 teaspoon finely chopped fresh thyme leaves

1 teaspoon finely chopped fresh rosemary leaves

³/₄ teaspoon ground black pepper

¹/₂ teaspoon red pepper flakes

¹/₄ teaspoon cayenne pepper

¹/₄ teaspoon powdered cloves

**You'll be amazed how much better homemade sausage tastes than store-bought. And it's simple to make.**

**1.** Combine all ingredients and chill 1 hour.

**2.** Preheat a grill to 350°F, or a skillet on your stove to medium heat. While grill is heating, form meat mixture into 2-inch round patties. Cook until juices run clear, about 3 minutes per side. Serve hot.

# SMOKED SAUSAGE AND EGG TACOS

MAKES 4 SERVINGS

2 tablespoons canola oil

¹/₂ pound smoked pork link sausage, in ¹/₂-inch dice

1 tablespoon chopped mild green chilis

1 tablespoon chopped green jalapeño pepper

4 large eggs

Salt and ground black pepper to taste

4 (6-inch) corn tortillas

4 tablespoons shredded Cheddar cheese

2 green onions, chopped thin

For serving: your favorite picante sauce

**1.** Heat oil in a heavy-bottomed skillet over the medium-high heat of a propane burner or a stove, and sauté sausage until it begins to brown, about 3 minutes. Add chopped chilis and jalapeño and sauté 1 more minute.

**2.** In a bowl, whisk the eggs and add them to the skillet. Season with salt and pepper. Stir the eggs until they are soft scramble. Taste for seasonings. Set aside and keep warm.

**3.** Heat a grill or skillet over high heat. Grill the tortillas quickly, until they are a tad charred on both sides, about 1 minute total. Divide the tortillas among 4 plates. Top each with a scoop of the cooked eggs, a tablespoon of cheese, and a portion of green onion. Drizzle on picante sauce and wrap tacos closed. Serve immediately.

# ANDOUILLE HASH

**Andouille is a seasoned coarse-grind smoked pork sausage. It's a must in chicken or wild duck gumbo. Its heavy smoke also adds outstanding flavor to smothered vegetables.**

**1.** Preheat a covered grill or an oven to 450°F. On a baking sheet, toss the potatoes with the olive oil, salt, and black pepper. Bake on indirect grill heat, covered, or in the oven until golden brown, 10–12 minutes.

**2.** While potatoes are cooking, heat a Dutch oven over the medium-high heat of a propane burner or your stove. Add canola oil, and when it's hot, add onion and jalapeño. Cook until onion begins to soften, 3–4 minutes.

**3.** Add the andouille, garlic powder, chili powder, smoked paprika, and cayenne. Cook until andouille is almost browned, about 4 minutes. Add the browned potatoes to the skillet, stir gently, and heat it all through. Scrape the hash onto a platter, top with green onion, and serve immediately.

2 large russet potatoes, skin on and in 1/2-inch dice

1/4 cup olive oil

1 teaspoon kosher salt

1 teaspoon freshly ground black pepper

2 tablespoons canola oil

1 small yellow onion, diced

1 jalapeño pepper, diced

1 pound andouille sausage, in 1/2-inch dice

1 teaspoon garlic powder

1/2 teaspoon ancho chili powder

1/2 teaspoon smoked paprika

1/4 teaspoon cayenne pepper

For serving: 1/4 cup chopped green onion

# BARBECUED SPARERIBS

MAKES 6-8 SERVINGS

3 slabs of St. Louis–style pork spareribs

1/2 cup Jay D's Louisiana Molasses Mustard (purchased or recipe page 184)

1 cup Jay D's Spicy & Sweet Barbecue Rub (purchased or recipe page 183, or your favorite commercial brand)

Pecan or cherry wood chips

1 1/2 cups apple juice

1 cup Jay D's Louisiana Barbecue Sauce, plus additional for serving (purchased or recipe page 186, or your favorite commercial brand)

One year my buddy Matt and I packed my "Monstrosity" barbecue pit into the bed of an old Toyota 4×4 pickup and drove 360 miles to Little Rock for the LSU game against Arkansas. After a fantastic weekend of tailgating and football, we woke up early, lit a hot fire in the barbecue pit, put in a couple of sparerib racks, and drove off for home. Somewhere around Lake Providence, Louisiana, the catalytic converter on the truck plugged up, and we had to pull over. While waiting for the white-hot converter to cool down enough to work on, we realized the smoke in the barbecue pit was dwindling. We also figured out we were parked next to a pecan grove. What luck! So we gathered fallen tree limbs and stoked the fire in our smoker. We eventually fixed the pickup enough to drive it, and all the way home we were billowing smoke from both the barbecue pit and the straight exhaust of the truck with no muffler. When we made it back to Baton Rouge, we decided to worry about the truck later, and took those ribs out of the smoker. They were outstanding.

**1.** Remove membranes from rib slabs and discard. Wash ribs well and pat dry with paper towels. Apply an even coating of molasses mustard to both sides of all 3 slabs. Generously coat everything with barbecue rub, letting the mustard act as an adhesive. Marinate rib racks at room temperature 30 minutes.

**2.** While ribs are marinating, soak the wood chips and prepare a covered grill for indirect heat, or set your oven at 300–325°F. If you're using a grill, throw the drained wood chips into the fire or into your wood basket. Place ribs over indirect heat and cook them until they get some nice smoke and a little char, about 1 1/2 hours. In the oven, bake without the wood chips for 1 1/2 hours.

**3.** Pour the apple juice into an aluminum foil pan or a heat-proof baking pan that's as long as the rib racks. Stand the ribs on their edges in the pans and cover with aluminum foil. Return to the grill and cover, or into your oven and

cook until ribs are tender, but not completely fall-off-the-bone, about one more hour. Slice into individual ribs and serve warm with barbecue sauce.

**To make ahead:** If you want to make the ribs the day before, allow the fully cooked ribs to cool at room temperature and wrap each rack individually in plastic wrap. To reheat, remove the plastic and place the cooked ribs over indirect heat, uncovered, on a grill set at medium-high heat, or in your oven at 350°F. Flip them over every few minutes, brushing each side with barbecue sauce each time you flip. Heat until the ribs are slightly caramelized and hot through the center. Should take about half an hour.

# GRILLED PORK CHOPS WITH SPICY PEACH CHUTNEY

MAKES 4 SERVINGS

3 (12-ounce) bottles slightly fruity wheat beer, divided

2 cups brown sugar, divided

2 tablespoons salt

2 tablespoons ground cinnamon

1 tablespoon ground black pepper

1 tablespoon allspice

1 bay leaf

4 thick cut pork chops

1/2 cup (1 stick) butter

2 shallots, finely chopped

2 fresh jalapeño peppers, finely chopped

1 garlic clove, finely chopped

2 fresh, ripe peaches, stones removed and finely chopped

Creole seasoning (purchased or recipe page 182)

In Louisiana, peaches grow best in the northern part of the state, around Ruston, where they're at their peak in June. Ruston peaches are as juicy and sweet as any you'll find anywhere.

**1.** Make a beer brine by pouring 2 bottles of beer into a large heavy saucepan. Place the pan on a propane burner or your stove and heat until it simmers. Add 1 1/2 cups brown sugar, salt, cinnamon, black pepper, allspice, and bay leaf. Heat until granular ingredients have dissolved. Remove from heat and let mixture come to room temperature.

**2.** Add the pork chops to the cooled brine, and allow them to soak at least an hour or two in the refrigerator. Let them come back to room temperature in the brine before grilling.

**3.** About 20 minutes before the pork is finished marinating, make the chutney. Over a propane burner or your stove set at medium heat, melt the butter in a large saucepan. Sauté the shallots in the butter. Once soft, add the jalapeños and garlic. Sauté until cooked down and soft, about 2 minutes, then add the chopped peaches. Continue to cook until the peaches are broken down, about 5 minutes. Add half of the remaining beer (drink the other half), the remaining 1/2 cup brown sugar, and Creole seasoning to taste. Let the pot of chutney simmer while you grill the pork chops.

**4.** Prepare a grill to medium heat, or place a heavy skillet over medium heat on your stove. Remove the pork chops from the brine and place on the grill over direct heat. Cook two minutes, then flip. Continue cooking, while flipping every 2–3 minutes. Cooking times vary depending on thickness of the chop and temperature of the grill. It will probably take 5–10 minutes per side. If you want to be sure the pork is cooked thoroughly yet still juicy, check the internal temperature with a probe thermometer. Current guidelines say that pork is safe to eat at an internal temperature of 140°F.

**5.** Remove the pork chops from the grill and allow them to rest a few minutes. Top each chop with the peach chutney and serve warm. This chutney has a kick, so if you bought a whole six-pack, now's the time to enjoy those last few beers.

# CRISPY PIG EAR SALAD WITH MOLASSES MUSTARD VINAIGRETTE

**MAKES 6 SERVINGS**

While ears aren't the most popular edible part of the pig, you'll be amazed at how flavorful they can be if you cook them right. The key to getting the proper crispy texture is to tender-cook them first, either by boiling or using some other low and slow technique. Then let the ears cool thoroughly, cut them into small strips, and crisp them in the fryer, like pork cracklins.

**1.** Halfway fill a Dutch oven with water and add the onions, celery, garlic, and 1 tablespoon salt. Bring to a rolling boil over a propane burner or your stove and add pig ears. Lower to a hard simmer and cook until pig ears are soft, about 2 hours. Remove pig ears and place in an ice bath. Let them sit until they're totally cooled through. You can fry them now or refrigerate them up to 24 hours.

**2.** Dry the ears well and slice into 1/4-inch strips. Add 2 inches vegetable oil to a deep fryer and heat both it and a covered grill to 375°F. Fry pig ear slices until very crispy and crunchy. Set aside on paper towels.

**3.** In a bowl, combine olive oil, remaining teaspoon salt, and black pepper. Coat carrots with the olive oil mixture and place them on the grill. Close the cover and cook until carrots are soft and have grill marks, about 6 minutes.

**4.** To serve, toss spinach and arugula in the amount of vinaigrette to your liking. Place a bed of greens on salad plates. Top with carrots, then the Gouda, then the crispy pig ears. Finish with a drizzle of vinaigrette and serve immediately.

Water

2 medium yellow onions, cut in half

4 ribs celery

6 cloves garlic, peeled

1 tablespoon, plus 1 teaspoon kosher salt

4 pig ears

Vegetable oil for frying

3 tablespoons olive oil

1 teaspoon coarsely ground black pepper

6 heirloom carrots, cut in half lengthwise

1 (10-ounce) bag baby spinach

1 (10-ounce) bag arugula

Molasses Mustard Vinaigrette (recipe follows)

2 cups finely grated smoked Gouda cheese

# MOLASSES MUSTARD VINAIGRETTE

MAKES ABOUT 1 CUP

A heaping ½ cup Jay D's Louisiana Molasses Mustard (purchased or recipe page 184)

3 tablespoons white balsamic vinegar

2 tablespoons Jay D's Blanc du Bois or other white wine

1 tablespoon salt

1 tablespoon white wine vinegar

⅓ cup extra virgin olive oil

Whisk everything together except the oil. Whisking continuously, slowly add the olive oil in a thin stream. Keep whisking until dressing is fully emulsified. Dressing keeps in the refrigerator in a tightly capped jar up to 3 days.

# BACON-WRAPPED PORK TENDERLOIN

MAKES 4-6 SERVINGS

2 (1- to 1½-pound) pork tenderloins, trimmed of excess fat and silverskin (silvery colored connective tissue)

2 tablespoons Cajun seasoning (purchased or recipe page 182)

12 strips raw bacon

Toothpicks

**Pork tenderloins dry out fast, so it's best to cook them quickly over high heat.**

**1.** Preheat a grill to 375°F, or your oven to 425°F. Rub tenderloins with Cajun seasoning. Wrap 6 strips of bacon around each tenderloin and secure with toothpicks.

**2.** Place pork onto hot grill over direct heat. Making a ¼ turn every 4–5 minutes, cook until the bacon is nicely brown and crisp and the pork's internal temperature reaches 140–145°F, about 18–20 minutes. If cooking in the oven, you don't have to turn it. Remove from heat and allow to rest 5 minutes. Cut into 1¼-inch slices and serve.

# COCHON DE LAIT (ROASTED WHOLE YOUNG PIG)

MAKES 20-50 SERVINGS, DEPENDING ON HOW YOU'RE SERVING IT

**1.** Using a meat saw, cut through the backbone at the neck and tail and lay the pig open flat. Combine the butter, hot sauce, wine, crab boil, Worcestershire sauce, and remaining 3/4 cup granulated garlic. Inject the front and rear pork hams and tenderloin with the seasoned butter mixture.

**2.** Season the pig extremely well inside and out with salt, black pepper, and granulated garlic. Lay sheets of wire mesh below and above the flattened pig. Secure the mesh all around with wire, so that the pig is tightly enclosed inside the mesh.

**3.** Make a hardwood fire in a dug pit, a very large barbecue pit, or a Cajun microwave. Mount the pig 3 to 4 feet away from the fire and cook it until the hams are 150°F and the shoulders are 170°F. Turn the pig over every hour and try to keep the fire going so that it produces a constant 250–300°F near the pig. It should take a little over 1 hour of cooking for every 10 pounds.

**4.** When the pig is done, its skin will be a nice crackly brown, the meat will fall off the bone, and the whole thing will be extremely hot. Wear thick gloves and get someone to help you transfer the pig in the mesh to a large table. Carefully remove the wire mesh and chop the pig into serving pieces, or shred it and make po'boys or sandwiches.

1 whole pig, 40–50 pounds, cleaned and dressed

Salt and ground black pepper

Granulated garlic for seasoning, plus 3/4 cup

2 cups melted salted butter

1 cup Louisiana-style hot sauce

1 cup white wine

1/2 cup liquid crab boil

1/2 cup Worcestershire sauce

A food injector for liquid seasoning

Wire mesh or clean concrete reinforcing wire, plus wire for trussing, all washed and cleaned thoroughly

Hardwood for making a fire

# TRIPLE-THREAT PULLED PORK

MAKES 4-6 SERVINGS (BEGIN A DAY AHEAD)

1 (8-pound) bone-in pork shoulder

1 cup Jay D's Louisiana Molasses Mustard (purchased or recipe page 184)

1 cup Jay D's Spicy & Sweet Barbecue Rub (purchased or recipe page 183, or your favorite commercial brand)

4 tablespoons kosher salt

2 cups applewood chips

2 cups Jay D's Louisiana Barbecue Sauce, plus additional for serving (purchased or recipe page 186, or your favorite commercial brand)

**This uncomplicated recipe makes a mountain of tender pulled pork that's good on sliders, in nachos, or as is.**

**1.** Dry pork well with paper towels. Coat with molasses mustard. Mix together the barbecue rub and the salt and apply liberally to all sides of the pork. Let it sit, uncovered, in the refrigerator overnight.

**2.** The day of cooking, soak the wood chips in water 30 minutes and heat a smoker to 225°F. Place wood chips in the smoker and place pork, fat side up, on a smoker grate. Cover and smoke until the meat is fall-apart tender, when the internal temperature reaches 190°F, about 1 hour per pound.

**3.** Take the pork off the smoker and let it cool slightly. Use gloves or tongs to pull pork apart and toss with barbecue sauce. Serve warm.

# SWEET POTATO CHIP AND PULLED-PORK NACHOS

MAKES 6 SERVINGS

**If you happen to have leftover pulled pork, try this party-friendly recipe with sweet potato chips that are restaurant-quality crisp.**

**1.** Over a propane burner or your stove, heat 2 inches oil in a deep fryer or Dutch oven to 300°F. Working in batches, drop in about 10 sweet potato slices at a time (depending on the size of your fryer), and partially cook 1–2 minutes. Transfer potatoes to a wire rack and let drain.

**2.** Set oil heat to 350°F. Working again in batches, drop partially cooked chips into oil until edges start to turn brown, about 1–2 minutes. Immediately remove from oil and drain on a paper towel–lined rack. Season with barbecue rub.

**3.** Heat a covered grill to medium-high, or heat up your oven's broiler. Layer fried sweet potatoes on a sheet pan. Top with pork, black beans, and cheese. Grill or broil until cheese melts. Top with avocado, sour cream, and jalapeños. Drizzle on barbecue sauce and serve immediately.

Vegetable oil for frying

2 large sweet potatoes, unpeeled and thinly sliced (a mandoline slicer does the job well)

Jay D's Spicy & Sweet Barbecue Rub (purchased or recipe page 183, or your favorite commercial brand)

1½ cups Triple Threat Pulled Pork (recipe page 58)

1 cup canned black beans, rinsed and blotted dry

1 cup shredded Monterrey Jack cheese

1 large, ripe avocado, sliced

½ cup sour cream

2 green jalapeño peppers, thinly sliced

Jay D's Louisiana Barbecue Sauce (purchased or recipe page 186, or your favorite commercial brand)

1 pound dried red kidney beans

1 pound smoked link pork sausage, sliced

2 tablespoons canola oil

1 large yellow onion, diced

1 large green bell pepper, seeded and diced

3 bay leaves

2 tablespoons Jay D's Spicy & Sweet Barbecue Rub (purchased or recipe page 183, or your favorite commercial brand)

1 tablespoon Cajun seasoning (purchased or recipe page 182)

1 teaspoon dried sage

1 bunch green onions, sliced

Salt and ground black pepper to taste

For serving: hot cooked rice (recipe page 166) and Louisiana-style hot sauce

# RED BEANS AND RICE WITH SMOKED PORK SAUSAGE

MAKES 8 SERVINGS (BEGIN A DAY AHEAD)

**1.** Rinse beans. Place in a bowl, cover by 2 inches water, and let soak at room temperature overnight.

**2.** In a large Dutch oven set over a propane burner or your stove, brown the sausage in the canola oil. Add the onion and bell pepper and sauté until onion is soft, about 5 minutes. Pour beans and the soaking water into the Dutch oven and bring to a simmer. Add bay leaves, barbecue rub, Cajun seasoning, and sage. Simmer, covered, until beans are tender, 1½–2 hours. Stir occasionally.

**3.** Thicken the liquid by using the back of a large spoon to mash about a cup of beans against the side of the pot. Stir in green onion and adjust seasoning. (Do not add salt before this point; it will toughen the beans.) Serve beans and sausage over hot rice, and splash on a few dashes of hot sauce.

# GRANNY'S DIRTY RICE

MAKES 8–10 SERVINGS

In the Cajun region of southwest Louisiana, this dish of ground-up meats and rice is called rice dressing. My Cajun grandmother's rice dressing was the stuff of legend.

1. Place chicken livers and gizzards into a food processor and pulse until coarsely ground. Set aside.

2. Over the medium-high heat of a propane burner or your stove, add canola oil to a heavy cast-iron Dutch oven and brown ground livers, gizzards, and pork. Make sure to render out all the fat from the meat. Pour off excess oil and add butter.

3. Add the onion, celery, bell pepper, and garlic, and sauté 5 minutes. Add 1 cup water to deglaze the pot. Simmer the meat and vegetables, covered, for an additional 5 minutes. Uncover and continue cooking until all the water evaporates.

4. Add remaining 4 cups water, salt, and black pepper and bring up to a boil. Stir in rice and bring back to a boil. Lower to a simmer and cook, covered, for 15 minutes. After 15 minutes, add the parsley and fold rice mixture from bottom to top. Put lid back on and simmer until rice is tender and liquid has evaporated, about 5–10 minutes. Remove from heat and let stand, covered, 5 minutes. Serve hot, garnished with green onion.

1 pound chicken livers

1 pound chicken gizzards

1 tablespoon canola oil

1 pound lean ground pork

1 tablespoon butter

2 medium onions, chopped

4 stalks celery, chopped

1 green bell pepper, chopped

8 cloves garlic, minced

5 cups water, divided

2 teaspoons kosher salt

Ground black pepper to taste

2 cups uncooked long-grain white rice

1 tablespoon chopped parsley

For serving: 1 cup chopped green onion

# PORK AND BRUSSELS SPROUT CAST-IRON BAKE

MAKES 4 SERVINGS

1 (1-pound) pork tenderloin

2 tablespoons smoked extra virgin olive oil, divided

2 tablespoons Jay D's Spicy & Sweet Barbecue Rub (purchased or recipe page 183, or your favorite commercial brand), divided

½ pound Brussels sprouts, halved lengthwise

Salt and ground black pepper to taste

**Smoked olive oil is getting easier and easier to find. If your local gourmet shop doesn't carry it, look it up online.**

**1.** Place a large cast-iron skillet directly over medium-high grill heat or on a hot stove burner. Rub pork with 1 tablespoon smoked olive oil and 1 tablespoon barbecue rub. Sear on all sides in the hot skillet. Remove from the skillet and set aside.

**2.** In the same skillet, toss Brussels sprouts with the remaining tablespoon of olive oil and barbecue rub. Sear sprouts, cut side down until nicely charred, about 3–4 minutes. Turn sprouts over and cook until just tender, about 3 more minutes. Sprinkle with salt and pepper.

**3.** Place the seared tenderloin on top of Brussels sprouts. For grill cooking, move skillet to indirect heat. Indoors, place in a 400°F oven. Close the grill cover and cook until internal temperature of pork reaches 145°F. Remove pan from grill and allow to sit 5 minutes. Slice pork and serve warm with sides of Brussels sprouts.

# BEEF & SHEEP
## (& ONE GOAT)

There's mouthwatering goodness in most cuts of lamb or beef cooked on a grill or smoker, and I've prepared just about all of it. Personally, beef is one of those meats I find myself craving, and I often cook it for celebrations. It's also one of the first things I learned to cook outdoors.

As a child in Texas, the goal of our family hunting trips was usually to bring home a trophy deer. Often, however, after spending the whole day seeking out the perfect buck, we'd arrive back at the camp empty-handed. To make sure we wouldn't starve, we always brought along cuts of beef. At dinnertime, while surrounded by barbed-wire fences, prickly pear cacti, and a sky full of stars, we'd gather fallen mesquite limbs and make a fire inside a giant metal ring. Then we'd wrap whole potatoes in foil and toss them onto the coals. When the potatoes were almost done, we'd top the live flames with a metal grill and char our steaks. I don't think I'll ever forget the smoky scent of beef sizzling over those crackling fires. I can't recall any other food triggering such an intensely happy memory.

### Vanishing Hoofstock

In 1950, Louisiana ranchers owned over 1.5 million head of cattle, and it was common for my grandparents' generation to see massive herds grazing behind fences along Louisiana's major highways. Back then, there were even hundreds of thousands of sheep. Today, ranchers are only raising around 788,000 cattle, and those beautiful pasture sightings are becoming more and more scarce.

As far back as the late 1700s, ranching was extremely common in Louisiana's southwest prairies. But, as with the plight of family farms, megaconglomerates have pretty much priced out small cattle and sheep producers. There is a local movement to raise grass-fed beef and sheep for slaughter, but the number of animals grown on these farms does not begin to compare with the bounteous days of the nineteenth and early twentieth centuries.

Jay prepares beef and much more on his *Cookin' Louisiane* show, filmed in his own professional-though-residential kitchen.

Louisiana was a leader in America's early cattle industry. It will probably surprise my Texas friends that America's first cattle drives did not clomp along the Old Chisholm Trail, but went along the Opelousas Trail, or the Beef Trail, through Louisiana's swamps and prairies. The first recorded cattle drive along the Opelousas Trail was in 1779. Little more than a trampled path, the route started in San Antonio, Texas, then branched out to the Sabine and Neches rivers (where many cattle drowned). From there it leads into Louisiana to areas I know well, the cities of Alexandria, Natchitoches, and Opelousas. The trail then generally turned south and followed what is now Interstate 10, to the port of New Orleans. The riders on those early cattle drives, which included many African Americans, worked hard in brutal conditions, winding herds through piney woods, grassy prairies, and the mucky Atchafalaya Swamp.

Those early cowboys did not have convenient auction markets along their trail. By the first half of the twentieth century, plenty of them dotted the state. Although not as plentiful today, there are still several large livestock markets around, and they typically auction off horses, hogs, sheep, goats, and cattle. Butcher shops, too, are not nearly as common as they used to be, but south Louisiana does have a few outstanding ones. When I cater large events, one of the slaughterhouses I routinely turn to is the Superette in Eunice, Louisiana, in Cajun country west of Baton Rouge. This wholesaler/retailer sits in the vicinity of what was the Old Opelousas Trail. They've been in business over fifty years and, as in days of old, they source from their network of local cattle ranchers and provide whatever a customer wants.

Fortunately, we have many other reminders of the golden days of cattle ranching, such as the name of the mascot for McNeese State University in Lake Charles, the Cowboys. Several Louisiana universities still have rodeo teams, and many communities host rodeos, including the much anticipated annual rodeo at Angola State Prison.

Even though the state's cattle business is diminishing, our area's love of beef is as strong as ever. Beef is often sizzling on my barbecue pits. It might be my much-requested brisket, or maybe tri-tip roast, flank steak, short ribs, or even meatloaf. I make a mean burger, respectable beef jerky, and in my cast-iron pot I cook beef stew and chili. I enjoy carrying on our state's tradition of cooking beef, and I like to think that those early Louisiana cowboys would be proud.

## General Custer

The side of me that loves hunting has always been drawn to farm life and to the animals that live on them. But since I've always lived in a city or suburb, it's been impossible to raise herds of living creatures. The closest I've come to raising something worth butchering was in Sugarland, Texas, where one of my high-school mentors, Mr. Jimmy Klemstein, taught extremely appealing classes in wildlife, hunting, boating safety, and animal science. In order for this city boy to justify taking his courses, I joined the club he worked with, the Future Farmers of America, later known as just the FFA.

To build up my farm creds and make a strong case for being elected FFA president, Mr. Klemstein recommended that I raise an animal and spend time at the district's shared barn. Choosing what I figured would be the easiest course of action, I decided to raise a goat.

So, I became the proud owner of a goat named General Custer, a scrappy little cuss with black-and-white hair. Custer was curious, full of energy, and smarter than me. And little had I realized it, but feeding and shoveling after a farm animal is hard work. Even so, I took to the little fellow. And I naturally thought he was handsome, so five months after I bought Custer, I talked my younger sister into showing him at the Houston Livestock Show and Rodeo. (I couldn't do the showing because I was academically ineligible. I hadn't given

**Jay slicing brisket hot off the smoker.**

a required speech for a class because I'd been away at an off-campus school event. I still bristle at that injustice.) Anyway, the day of the livestock show, General Custer dragged my sister around the arena, and to my shocked surprise he didn't place.

That same weekend, I sold him to a nice man with a real farm in the country. And I know what you're thinking: "Yo, Jay. General Custer would have made awesome cabrito." Truth is, I'd grown too attached. I don't give a second thought to bagging a deer, a wild boar, or a wild duck, but there's no way I'm going to eat a buddy. So, even though he'd lost at the livestock show, General Custer ended up a winner—he got the chance to lead a longer and happier life.

In the end, I served two years as my FFA chapter's reporter and my senior year as chapter president. I also learned a valuable lesson, that taking care of farm animals is a chore. I now have a greater appreciation for ranchers and their work. And I am grateful that the fat beefsteaks and lamp chops I enjoy are conveniently available at the butcher shop and grocery store.

# MARINATED AND GRILLED NEW YORK STRIP STEAKS

MAKES 4 SERVINGS

I've been grilling steaks so long I can easily tell when they're done by pressing them with my finger. If you're not familiar with the finger test and you want to be absolutely sure you don't overcook an expensive piece of meat, by all means, invest in a probe meat thermometer.

**1.** Pat steaks dry with a paper towel and prick all over with a fork. Mix marinade ingredients together in a large resealable food-safe plastic bag or in a large shallow pan. Add steaks to marinade, seal tightly, and refrigerate 1–2 hours.

**2.** Take steaks out of the refrigerator 1 hour before ready to cook. When ready to cook, prepare a grill for medium-high heat. Grill steaks directly over heat to desired doneness, flipping twice. If you're not sure if your steaks are done, probe with a meat thermometer. (Rare is bright red in the middle, 120–130°F; medium rare is a hint of red in the middle, 130–135°F; medium is light pink in the middle, 140–150°F. I don't cook tender steaks any more than medium rare, but if you like them cooked more than that, go for it.)

**3.** Allow steaks to sit 5 minutes so that they retain their juices. Remember, residual heat continues to cook them, and their internal temperature may rise as much as five degrees. Transfer steaks to warm serving plates.

4 (8-ounce) New York strip steaks

Vinaigrette Marinade:

1/2 cup Jay D's Louisiana Molasses Mustard (purchased or recipe page 184)

1/3 cup extra virgin olive oil

3 tablespoons white balsamic vinegar

3 tablespoons dry white wine

1 tablespoon white wine vinegar

1 tablespoon salt

# GRILLED RIB EYES WITH HERB BUTTER

MAKES 4 RIB EYE STEAKS

4 (10-ounce) Angus beef rib eye steaks

Kosher salt and freshly ground black pepper

Herb Butter (recipe follows)

**1.** Take steaks out of the refrigerator 1 hour before cooking.

**2.** Heat a grill to medium-high. Season steaks with salt and black pepper. Grill directly over heat to desired doneness, flipping twice. If you're not sure if your steaks are done, probe with a meat thermometer. (Rare, bright red in the middle, 120–130°F; medium rare, hint of red in the middle, 130–135°F; medium, light pink in the middle, 140–150°F.)

**3.** Allow cooked steaks to sit 5 minutes so that they retain their juices. Transfer steaks to warm plates. Top them with a slice of herb butter and dig in.

1 cup (2 sticks) unsalted butter, softened

1 tablespoon Roasted Garlic (recipe follows)

1½ teaspoons kosher salt

1 teaspoon freshly ground black pepper

1 teaspoon minced shallots

1 teaspoon minced fresh parsley

¾ teaspoon minced fresh rosemary

¼ teaspoon minced fresh sage

# HERB BUTTER

MAKES 1¼ CUPS

Combine all ingredients. Roll the herb butter in plastic wrap to form a 1½-inch diameter log. Refrigerate until ready to serve. (Can be made a day ahead.)

# ROASTED GARLIC

**Mashed roasted garlic is great in any kind of savory sauce. The whole roasted cloves also make a fantastic side dish. Just squeeze out the sweet golden-brown garlic and enjoy.**

4 large heads of garlic

2 tablespoons olive oil

Salt

**1.** Prepare one side of a covered grill for medium heat, or your oven to 350°F. Cut the garlic heads in half crosswise. Place them in the middle of a large doubled sheet of aluminum foil. Sprinkle the cut tops of garlic halves with oil and salt. Crimp the foil closed over the garlic.

**2.** Place the packet on the grill's warming rack over direct heat, or over indirect heat on the main grill. Close the cover, and cook until the cloves are soft and turning brown, about 30–45 minutes. Takes about the same amount of time in the oven.

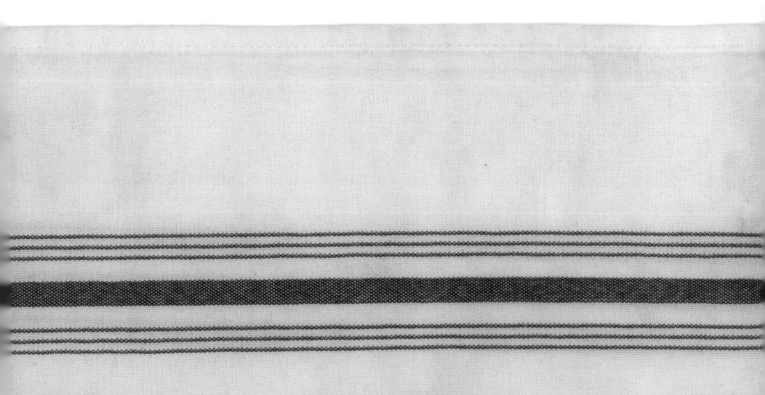

# SLOW-COOKED BEEF BRISKET

MAKES 8 SERVINGS

1 (4-pound) beef brisket, flat section, first-cut, trimmed of excess fat

10 cloves garlic, peeled

Kosher salt and ground black pepper

Your favorite low-sodium seasoning rub

Water

**1.** Preheat one side of a covered grill to 375°F, or your oven to 350°F. Cut 10 small slits throughout the brisket and stuff each slit with one clove of garlic. Liberally season brisket with salt, black pepper, and seasoning rub.

**2.** Put brisket in a heat-proof pan with edges at least as high as the flat brisket. Add water to the pan until it comes halfway up the brisket. Cover the pan with foil, place over the cool part of the grill, and cover the grill. In the oven, cook 1 hour, then lower heat to 300°F. Grill or bake until the brisket falls apart easily, about 5 hours. Serve sliced, or shred the brisket for tacos or sandwiches.

# COFFEE-AND-CHILI-RUBBED TRI-TIP

MAKES 6–8 SERVINGS

2-pound beef tri-tip roast (bottom sirloin), trimmed of silverskin (silvery colored connective tissue)

3 tablespoons canola oil

Salt and ground black pepper

1 cup Jay D's Coffee Chile Rub (purchased or recipe page 183)

At my restaurant, Gov't Taco, chefs Aimee Tortorich and Therese Schneider developed a unique chili rub made with the single-origin coffee that I sell. In certain dishes, such as this one, coffee adds an unparalleled depth of flavor.

**1.** Take the beef out of the refrigerator 1 hour before cooking. Preheat one side of a grill to 375°F. Rub beef with canola oil and liberally season all over with salt and pepper. Massage the coffee rub into the tri-tip. Place the meat on the hottest part of the grill and sear one side well, 6 to 8 minutes. Flip the meat and sear the other side well, 5 to 6 minutes.

**2.** Move the meat to the cool part of the grill. Cook 8 minutes. Flip and cook until an inserted meat thermometer reaches 130°F, medium rare, and that should take 5 to 8 minutes.

**3.** Remove meat from the grill and let rest 5 minutes. Slice meat against the grain and serve warm.

# BARBECUED MEATLOAF

MAKES 6 SERVINGS

1. Preheat a covered grill or your oven to 350°F. In a large cast-iron skillet set over a propane burner or your stove, melt the butter over medium heat. Add onion, celery, bell pepper, green onion, garlic, Tabasco, Cajun seasoning, salt, and Worcestershire sauce. Sauté, stirring occasionally and scraping up bottom of pan, until the mixture starts sticking excessively, about 6 minutes.

2. Stir in evaporated milk and ketchup, and cook an additional 2 minutes, stirring occasionally. Remove from heat and cool to room temperature.

3. In a mixing bowl, use your hands to mix together the cooled vegetable mixture, ground beef, ground pork, breadcrumbs, and eggs. Shape mixture into a free-form loaf, packing tightly. Place on a well-greased or parchment-lined cookie sheet.

4. Place cookie sheet on the cool side of the covered, preheated grill or in the oven. Cook 1 hour and 10 minutes. Glaze with the barbecue sauce and cook until the meatloaf reaches an internal temperature of 160°F. Should take a total of 1½–2 hours. Slice and serve warm.

5 tablespoons unsalted butter

1 cup chopped onion

½ cup chopped celery

½ cup chopped bell pepper

½ cup chopped green onion

5 cloves garlic, minced

1½ tablespoons Tabasco sauce

1 heaping tablespoon Cajun seasoning (purchased or recipe page 182)

1 tablespoon kosher salt

1 tablespoon Worcestershire sauce

½ cup evaporated milk

½ cup ketchup

1½ pounds ground beef

½ pound ground pork

1 cup fine, dry breadcrumbs

2 large eggs, beaten

¾ cup Jay D's Louisiana Barbecue Sauce (purchase or recipe page 186, or your favorite commercial brand)

# BARBECUED MEATBALLS

MAKES 2 TO 3 DOZEN, 1-INCH MEATBALLS

1 large onion, minced

3 cloves garlic, minced

1 teaspoon olive oil

1 pound lean ground beef

1 large egg, lightly beaten

1 tablespoon Jay D's Spicy & Sweet Barbecue Rub (purchased or recipe page 183, or your favorite commercial brand)

1½ cups Jay D's Louisiana Barbecue Sauce (purchased or recipe page 186, or your favorite commercial brand)

9 ounces apricot pepper jelly

**1.** Preheat a grill to 350°F, or your oven to 400°F. Meanwhile, in a small sauté pan, sauté onion and garlic with olive oil until onion is soft, about 5 minutes. Set aside to cool.

**2.** Mix together ground beef, egg, barbecue rub, and cooked onion and garlic. Roll mixture into 1-inch meatballs and place on a sheet pan. Cook meatballs over direct heat on the hot grill or in the oven, turning occasionally, until slightly browned, about 10 minutes.

**3.** In a saucepan set over the medium-high heat of a propane burner or your stove, mix together barbecue sauce and pepper jelly. Bring to a simmer. Add meatballs to sauce and continue to simmer for 15 minutes. Serve meatballs and sauce warm.

# BARBECUED CHILI

MAKES 8 SERVINGS

**1.** Heat a Dutch oven over medium propane or stove heat. Brown the beef, stirring occasionally, for 10 minutes. Remove the beef from the pot with a slotted spoon and set aside. Discard all but 2 tablespoons of the fat.

**2.** In the same pot, heat the two reserved tablespoons fat over medium-high heat and sauté the onion, bell peppers, garlic, serrano, and jalapeño. When vegetables are beginning to soften, after about 7 minutes, add the andouille and cook until it starts to brown, about 5 minutes.

**3.** Stir in the beef, beer, and barbecue rub and simmer 5 minutes. Add the oregano, chili powder, coriander, and cumin. Stir and simmer another 5 minutes.

**4.** Add the barbecue sauce and simmer until slightly thick, 10–20 minutes. Serve warm in bowls and offer an assortment of toppings.

2 pounds ground beef chuck (80/20)

1 medium yellow onion, diced

1 red bell pepper, diced

1 green bell pepper, diced

6 cloves garlic, minced

1 serrano pepper, seeded and diced

1 jalapeño pepper, seeded and diced

1/2 pound andouille, diced

1 1/2 cups dark beer

1/2 cup Jay D's Spicy & Sweet Barbecue Rub (purchased or recipe page 183, or your favorite commercial brand)

1 tablespoon dried Mexican oregano

2 teaspoons chili powder

1 teaspoon coriander

1 teaspoon cumin

1 1/2 cups Jay D's Louisiana Barbecue Sauce (purchased or recipe page 186, or your favorite commercial brand)

For serving: grated Cheddar cheese, chopped green onion, sour cream, corn chips, rice, tortilla chips, or anything your heart desires

2 tablespoons canola oil

2 pounds beef stew meat

Salt and ground black pepper

2 cups diced bell pepper

1 cup diced onion

1 cup diced carrots

Kernels of corn cut from 1 large ear

1/4 cup seeded and diced jalapeño pepper, or to taste

2 tablespoons tomato paste

1 tablespoon minced garlic

1 (28-ounce) can tomato sauce

1 (15-ounce) can diced tomatoes

5 tablespoons Jay D's Coffee Chile Rub (purchased or recipe page 183)

2 tablespoons chili powder

1 tablespoon balsamic vinegar

1/4 teaspoon cayenne pepper

1 1/4 cups canned black beans, drained and rinsed

1 cup chicken stock

For serving: lime wedges, diced avocado, and chopped cilantro

# CHUNKY BEEF AND BLACK BEAN CHILI

MAKES 4-6 SERVINGS

**This is a one-pot meal the whole family will enjoy.**

**1.** In a Dutch oven set over the medium-high heat of a propane burner or stove, heat oil until hot and sear beef with salt and pepper to taste. To prevent steaming, brown in small batches. Remove beef from pan and set aside.

**2.** To the same pot add bell pepper, onion, carrots, corn kernels, jalapeño, and tomato paste. Cook over medium heat 6 minutes, stirring frequently. Add garlic and cook until fragrant, about 30 seconds.

**3.** Add tomato sauce, diced tomatoes, Chile rub, chili powder, balsamic vinegar, and cayenne, and bring to a boil. Add black beans and chicken stock; then bring back to a boil. Reduce heat to a simmer and cook, covered, until beef is tender, 1–1 1/2 hours. Garnish with lime wedges, diced avocado, and cilantro. Serve hot in individual bowls.

# SLOPPY JOES

MAKES 4 SERVINGS

**Such sweet memories from my childhood, and a good party food for today.**

**1.** Set a large skillet over medium-high propane or stove heat and add 1 tablespoon olive oil. When oil is hot, add beef and Cajun seasoning. Sauté until beef is brown, about 5 minutes. Remove beef from pan and set aside.

**2.** Add remaining tablespoon olive oil to skillet and sauté vegetables until soft. Add beef back to pan, along with barbecue sauce and water. Bring to a boil, lower to a simmer, and cook, uncovered, until liquid is reduced and slightly thickened, about 20 minutes. Serve warm between hamburger buns.

2 tablespoons olive oil, divided

1 pound lean ground beef

1 teaspoon Cajun seasoning (purchased or recipe page 182)

1/2 cup chopped onion

1/4 cup chopped green bell pepper

1/4 cup chopped red bell pepper

1 cup Jay D's Louisiana Barbecue Sauce (purchased or recipe page 186, or your favorite commercial brand)

2/3 cup water

For serving: hamburger buns

# CAJUN CHEESEBURGER WITH GRILLED ONIONS AND PRALINE BACON

MAKES 6 HAMBURGERS

1 large yellow onion

1 tablespoon canola oil

Kosher salt

1 pound regular sliced bacon

3 tablespoons unsalted butter

1/2 cup light brown sugar

2 pounds 80/20 ground beef

Cajun seasoning (purchased or recipe page 182)

7 ounces Cheddar cheese, grated

6 hamburger buns

For serving: potato chips and Jay D's Louisiana Molasses Mustard (purchased or recipe page 184)

When I was on *Food Network Star,* this is the recipe I made on the episode called "Food Truck Throwdown." It was also in this contest that I created the Louisiana Molasses Mustard I now sell commercially. Arnold Myint, a restaurateur from Nashville, and I gave our two-chef team the name Asian Cajun Burger Boys, and we claimed victory in this challenge.

**1.** Peel the onion and slice it into thin rings. In a large bowl, toss onion with canola oil and 1/2 teaspoon salt. On a grill or a stove, heat a flattop grill or a cast-iron skillet over high heat. Sauté the onions until caramelized and soft. Set aside.

**2.** Cut bacon strips into thirds crossways. Cook bacon on the same grill you used for the onions until the fat is rendered and bacon is crispy. Transfer bacon to a rimmed baking sheet and leave the bacon drippings on the grill.

**3.** In a medium saucepan over medium heat, melt the butter and add the brown sugar. Cook until sugar is dissolved and bubbly, about 3–4 minutes. Carefully pour the mixture over the bacon. Use tongs or a large spoon to stir bacon around in the sauce. Toss until well coated and set aside.

**4.** Form the ground beef into 6 patties that are roughly 1/3 pound each. Sprinkle each patty on both sides with Cajun seasoning. Cook the burgers in the bacon drippings on the hot grill or in your skillet. For medium, cook about 3 minutes per side, and 4 minutes per side for medium-well. The last 30 seconds, top each burger with cheese.

**5.** Toast the burger buns on the grill or in your oven. Place the burgers on the bottoms of the buns. Top with the grilled onions, praline bacon, and top parts of the buns. Serve with sides of potato chips and Molasses Mustard.

# IRISH BEEF STEW

MAKES 4–6 SERVINGS

A sizable part of New Orleans's population originated in Ireland. The Louisiana version of traditional Irish stew is made with beef, not lamb or mutton, and it's popular throughout the southern part of the state. We Cajuns, of course, serve it—and anything that makes a scintilla of gravy—over rice.

**1.** Toss beef with salt and pepper. Heat a heavy-bottomed Dutch oven over the medium-high heat of a propane burner or stove and add oil. Sear beef until golden brown.

**2.** Add onion, celery, and diced carrot, and sauté 3–5 minutes. Sprinkle on flour and stir constantly until flour is slightly toasted, about 3 minutes.

**3.** Add stock, beer, tomato paste, Chile rub, and garlic. Simmer, uncovered, until meat is just tender, about 1–2 hours. Stir occasionally.

**4.** Add potatoes and carrot and parsnip rounds and simmer another 30 minutes. Serve over rice garnished with chopped parsley.

3 pounds beef stew meat

Salt and ground black pepper to taste

2 tablespoons olive oil

2 cups finely diced onion

2 cups finely diced celery

1 cup diced carrot

2 tablespoons all-purpose flour

1 quart beef stock

12 ounces stout beer

3 ounces tomato paste

2 tablespoons Jay D's Coffee Chile Rub (purchased or recipe page 183)

1 tablespoon minced garlic

4 cups fingerling or red potatoes

3-cup mixture of carrots and parsnips, cut into 1/2-inch rounds

For serving: hot cooked rice (recipe page 166) and chopped parsley

# OXTAIL STEW

5 pounds oxtail, cut into large pieces

Salt and ground black pepper

1/3 cup olive oil, plus 1 tablespoon

2 medium leeks, white and tender green parts, chopped

2 stalks celery, diced

4 medium carrots, chopped

3 sprigs fresh thyme

3 sprigs fresh rosemary

3 bay leaves

4 cloves garlic, minced

2 tablespoons all-purpose flour

5 medium tomatoes

1 quart beef broth

1 cup red wine

1 bunch green onions, chopped

For serving: hot cooked rice (recipe page 166)

**Oxtails originally came from real oxen, but the ones you find in today's meat cases come from steer tails. This cut has lots of bone and fat marbling, and it is tough. But when oxtails are braised, they practically melt in your mouth and are full of meaty flavor.**

**1.** Preheat a grill to high heat, or a heavy skillet set over medium-high stove heat. Season oxtail pieces with salt and pepper and toss in 1/3 cup olive oil. Roast the pieces over direct grill heat, covered, or in the skillet until golden brown. Remove and let cool.

**2.** Preheat a Dutch oven over medium propane or stove heat. Add the remaining tablespoon of olive oil and sauté the leeks, celery, and carrots 6 minutes. Add the thyme, rosemary, and bay leaves, and continuing sautéing 10 minutes. Add garlic and sauté until fragrant, about 1 minute.

**3.** Sprinkle the vegetable mixture with flour and cook, stirring constantly, 2 minutes. Add tomatoes, broth, and wine and simmer briskly a few minutes, scraping up any accumulated bits from the bottom. Add the oxtail and any accumulated juices. Cover, move the pot to a place on the grill where it will simmer, or put it in your oven at 325°F. Cook until fork tender, about 2–3 hours. Stir frequently to avoid burning at the bottom of the pot. Add water as necessary.

**4.** Remove oxtail pieces to a plate to cool. Discard thyme, rosemary sprigs, and bay leaves. Skim off the fat. When oxtails are cool enough to handle, pick the meat off the bones and return to the pot. Discard the bones. Rewarm stew over medium heat, stirring occasionally. Check to see if it needs salt and pepper, and stir in green onions. Serve over rice.

# VEAL LIVER AND ONIONS

MAKES 4-6 SERVINGS

1. Place liver in a bowl with the milk. Cover and marinate in the refrigerator up to 2 hours.

2. In a large shallow bowl mix together flour and Cajun seasoning. Shake milk off the pieces of liver and dredge in the flour mixture. In a cast-iron skillet set over the medium-high heat of a propane burner or stove, heat canola oil until hot. Brown liver a few minutes on each side. Set liver aside.

3. Over medium-high heat, deglaze the skillet with 1/2 cup wine until the liquid is mostly reduced. Add butter and reduce heat to medium. When butter is melted, sauté onion until translucent, about 7–8 minutes.

4. Return liver to skillet. Add remaining 1/2 cup wine, cover, and cook 20 minutes over medium-low heat. The sauce should be slightly thickened and the onions completely soft. Serve liver warm, topped with onions and sauce.

2 pounds sliced veal liver, rinsed under cool water

2 cups whole milk

1 cup all-purpose flour

1/2 teaspoon Cajun seasoning (purchased or recipe page 182)

2 tablespoons canola oil

1 cup Jay D's Blanc Du Bois Wine, or your favorite dry white wine, divided

1 tablespoon unsalted butter

1 sweet yellow onion, sliced

# GRILLED LAMB CHOPS

MAKES 4 SERVINGS

1. In a mortar and pestle or a blender, combine garlic, oil, salt, pepper, and rosemary until it forms a coarse paste. Rub on both sides of lamb chops and refrigerate 30 minutes to an hour.

2. When ready to cook, remove chops from the refrigerator 30 minutes ahead of time. Meanwhile, prepare a charcoal grill for indirect heat, the hot side at high heat. Grill chops over direct heat until both sides have a nice char, 2–3 minutes total. Move to the cool side of the grill and cook, brushing occasionally with Molasses Mustard, until insides reach 130°F for medium-rare, 135–140°F for medium, and 145–150°F for medium-well. This should take about 6–8 more minutes. Let chops sit 5 minutes before serving.

2 cloves garlic

2 tablespoons olive oil

1 teaspoon kosher salt

1/2 teaspoon coarsely ground black pepper

1/2 teaspoon minced fresh rosemary

8 loin lamb chops, thick cut

Jay D's Louisiana Molasses Mustard (purchased or recipe page 184)

A whole leg of lamb, boneless
(around 3–4 pounds)

Fruity wood chips for smoking,
such as cherry, apple, or peach

Butcher's twine

Brine:

3 quarts water

1/2 cup kosher salt

1/4 cup sugar

2 teaspoons curing salt,
known as "pink salt"

6 garlic cloves, rough chopped

1/4 cup pickling spice
(recipe follows)

1 tablespoon juniper berries,
crushed

Dry Rub (mix everything together):

2 tablespoons coarsely ground
black pepper

1 tablespoon ground coriander

1 teaspoon ground mustard seed

1 teaspoon ground cumin

1 teaspoon dried, ground rosemary

# LAMB PASTRAMI

MAKES 8-10 SERVINGS (BEGIN 3-4 DAYS AHEAD)

**1.** If your butcher did not butterfly-cut the lamb, do so, so that the whole thing lays flat. Put it back in the refrigerator.

**2.** In a pan, bring 1 quart water to a boil. Add the salts and sugar and stir until everything is dissolved. Remove from heat and add remaining 2 quarts water, garlic, pickling spice, and the juniper berries. Refrigerate the brine until it is completely cool. Add the leg of lamb to the cold brine, making sure that the lamb remains totally submerged. Cover the container and refrigerate 3 days.

**3.** The day of cooking, mix the dry rub. Soak the wood chips in water 30 minutes. While the wood is soaking, remove the lamb from the brine. Rinse and pat dry. Liberally coat all sides of the lamb with the dry rub and work it in with your hands. Roll the lamb jellyroll style or into a ball, and tie it tightly together with butcher's twine. Dust the outside of the lamb with a little more of the dry rub.

**4.** Prepare a smoker with the soaked wood to 250°F. Smoke the lamb until it reaches an internal temperature of 165°F, about 3 hours. Allow to cool completely. To serve, cut into very thin slices.

2 whole dried chilies
(ancho or chipotle work great)

2 cinnamon sticks

4 bay leaves

1/4 cup black peppercorns, toasted

1/4 cup whole allspice

1/4 cup whole cloves

1/4 cup whole mustard seeds

1 tablespoon coriander seeds,
toasted

1 tablespoon cumin seeds, toasted

# PICKLING SPICE

MAKES ABOUT 1½ CUPS

**In addition to lamb pastrami, you can use this spice blend to pickle cucumbers, green beans, carrot sticks, beets, and onions.**

Discard stems and seeds of chilies. Crush or chop chilies, cinnamon sticks, and bay leaves into 1/4-inch pieces. Stir them together with remaining ingredients, and you now have an economical batch of pickling spice blend. Store it in an airtight container.

# GOAT MOLE

MAKES 6 SERVINGS

**Serve this mole sauce in a bowl with rice or inside warm, soft tortillas. Shredded, the goat meat makes a dynamite taco filling.**

**1.** Preheat a covered grill or oven to 350°F. Pull out the stems and remove the seeds from all chilis. Slice open and flatten the larger peppers. Place the chilis on a skillet or baking sheet and place in covered grill until fragrant, about 5 minutes. In your oven, this might take 10 minutes. Remove peppers from heat and allow to cool. Finely chop the chilis and set aside.

**2.** Season the goat with salt and pepper and set aside. Spread sesame seeds and chopped pecans on a baking sheet together and toast until the sesame turns brown, about 10–12 minutes. Place the sesame seeds and pecans aside.

**3.** Place a large, deep cast-iron skillet or Dutch oven over the medium-high heat of a propane burner or your stove. Add the peanut oil. Sweat the onion 5 minutes. Add the chopped chilis, along with salt and pepper to taste. Reduce the heat to medium and cook 3 minutes, stirring often with a wooden spoon or spatula.

**4.** Add the chocolate, garlic, cinnamon, and cloves, and stir until chocolate is melted. Stir in the chicken stock and beer. Add the tomato, tomatillo, raisins, sugar, thyme, toasted sesame seeds, and toasted pecans. Simmer 30 minutes. Taste and adjust with salt and pepper if necessary. You now have a chunky mole sauce. Remove the skillet from heat and allow it to cool slightly.

**5.** Place the mole in a blender or large food processor and puree until smooth, about 1 minute. Return the mole to the skillet and bring to a simmer. Place the seasoned goat into the mole in one layer, making sure that each piece is coated with sauce. Braise the goat in the sauce in the covered grill or in your oven until tender, 30–45 minutes, flipping each piece once through the cooking process.

**6.** Remove the skillet from the heat and serve pieces of goat covered in sauce. For tacos, transfer the goat to a hard work surface or baking pan. When the meat is cool, separate it from the bones. Shred the meat and return it to the mole sauce. Reheat, spoon over hot rice or into warm tortillas, and garnish with cilantro and chopped onion.

1 dried chipotle chili

1 dried ancho chili

1 dried mulato chili

1 dried pasilla chili

2 pounds goat stew meat, cut into 1-inch cubes

Kosher salt and freshly ground black pepper

2 tablespoons sesame seeds

2 tablespoons chopped pecans

3 tablespoons peanut oil

1 medium yellow onion, finely chopped

4 tablespoons (about 1.5 ounces) chopped semisweet chocolate or Mexican chocolate

2 cloves garlic, minced

1/4 teaspoon ground cinnamon

1/8 teaspoon ground cloves

3 cups chicken stock

1 cup beer

1 large ripe tomato or 3 to 4 plum tomatoes, roughly chopped

1 tomatillo, husked, rinsed, and roughly chopped

2 tablespoons golden raisins

1 tablespoon sugar

1/2 teaspoon dried thyme

For serving: hot cooked rice (recipe page 166) or flour tortillas (purchased or recipe page 175), and cilantro and chopped onion.

# SEAFOOD

I have a lust for fish and shellfish, which makes south Louisiana an outstanding place for me to live. According to the Louisiana Seafood Market and Promotions Board, we're the nation's second-largest seafood supplier, just behind Alaska. One of every seventy Louisiana jobs is related to the seafood industry, which has an annual economic impact of $2.4 billion.

The people who catch fish for a living are a breed apart, there's no doubt about that. Their hours are long. The boats and docks are hot and messy. Hurricanes can shut things down for months, and there's an increasing struggle against competition from cheap farm-raised foreign imports. But in spite of these challenges, most fishermen wouldn't want to live any other way. Here's an overview of what these dedicated, hard-working folks sell commercially.

**Crawfish:** In the spring, one of my most requested catering gigs is for crawfish boils. In 2019, this was the dish that I challenged Bobby Flay to on an episode of the Food Network's *Beat Bobby Flay,* and I beat him on his own show! In Louisiana, crawfish are plentiful, and they make a logical choice for feeding large groups outdoors. These events are super-casual, with lots of paper towels and beer accompanying piles of steaming hot crawfish, potatoes, and corn all dumped onto newspaper-covered picnic tables. If hosts want to be fancy, they might splurge for individual plastic trays and packaged moist towelettes. Nobody beats Louisiana when it comes to producing and consuming crawfish. The swampy Atchafalaya Basin is the world's best habitat for growing them, and those beady-eyed crustaceans are everywhere. (After a hard spring rain in southwest Louisiana, it's not unusual to find crawfish crawling all over yards and on roads.) Over 800 commercial fishermen catch crawfish in the wilds of the Atchafalaya, but the bulk comes from the over 1,000 farmers who raise them in off-season rice fields. Louisiana farmers produce 110 million pounds of crawfish each year, and we eat about 90 percent of that total right here at

Boiled crabs.

home. The live crawfish season starts in January and goes through June. Fortunately, we can buy frozen cleaned tails year-round.

**Crabs:** Whether they're swimming in cheese in au gratin, boiled in highly seasoned water, or an ingredient in a holiday seafood dressing, I'm always up for crabs. The variety we eat in Louisiana are blue crabs, and we catch more of them than any other state. Maybe that's because the crabs off our coast bite virtually any day of the year. If it's off-season for shrimp or finfish, commercial fishermen know they'll be able to catch crabs. Well, sort of. In order to ease the pressure on the blue crab stock, in 2017, the state passed a regulation closing the commercial crab season for a month during late February and early March. Soft-shell crabs are plentiful from May through August. Most commercial soft-shell crabs are farm-raised. They're nurtured in enclosed tanks and watched vigilantly, until the exoskeleton of a freshly molten crab begins to harden. The still-limp crab is then quickly plucked out of the tank and it's ready to sell. I'm glad someone goes through all that trouble; a fried seafood platter wouldn't seem complete without a whole, crispy soft-shell crab.

**Oysters:** When I eat out, I often scour the appetizer list for something that revolves around a perfectly fried or chargrilled oyster. Fortunately, Louisiana has a robust oyster industry, and we can buy them freshly shucked in grocery stores and in restaurants year-round. Our oyster business owes much to the Croatian fishermen who settled along the Gulf Coast in the nineteenth century. Not only did this population catch all types of fresh seafood to supply metropolitan New Orleans, but they created a sophisticated oyster industry that, to this day, still uses their harvesting inventions. The success of Louisiana's modern commercial oyster crops depends tremendously on weather and climate conditions. There was a huge setback in late 2005, when it was feared that hurricanes Katrina and Rita had ruined the business for decades. In 2010, with the industry still recovering, there was another major setback, when the BP oil spill devastated our coastal environment. Against every odd imaginable, however, the oyster beds came back. In 2019, however, they faced their latest threat, fresh water pouring into oyster bed regions from the Bonne Carre Spillway, which was opened a record second time to help relieve the swollen Mississippi River. Even with all these challenges, our tenacious oyster farmers still manage to produce 42 percent of the nation's oysters. That's half of what's harvested out of the Gulf of Mexico.

**Shrimp:** Aside from crabs and crawfish, another go-to Louisiana crustacean is shrimp. Even the pickiest of eaters seem to like them. Shrimp are extremely versatile, and they go well in any kind of gumbo, étouffée, savory pie, po'boy, or salad. As with so much of our seafood, most large grocery stores sell wild, fresh Louisiana shrimp, and it always seems to be available. Our state's shrimping industry is extremely important, providing fifteen thousand jobs, with an annual $1.3 billion impact, and we sell a whopping 73 percent of the nation's shrimp. Shrimp boats and the love of the occupation tend to be handed down through families. Lately, Louisiana's Vietnamese population has carved out a large presence in this industry. Depending on the size of the captain's boat, shrimp are caught in inland or coastal waters or much farther out, in deep federal waters. The sight of a sailing shrimp lugger with its butterfly nets outstretched is a thing of beauty. And the sight of a platter of whole, perfectly boiled shrimp isn't bad to look at either.

**Finfish:** Louisiana ranks second in the harvest of finfish and, surprisingly, 97 percent of that total is menhaden, locally known as pogies. Pogies are small oily fish that run in gigantic schools. They're caught offshore in large nets, called purse seines, and are processed into meal, fertilizer, and fish oil. (That fish oil vitamin you take might come from Gulf of Mexico pogie.) Seasonal wild fish for the table, however, are easy to find in restaurants and seafood markets, as is locally farmed catfish. With the national increased demand for wild-caught fish, I'm finding it much easier to buy commercially sold tuna, red snapper, flounder, mahi mahi, black drum, grouper, and sheepshead. There's also a small but exciting availability of more exotic species, such as the invasive lionfish.

## Fishing for Fun

I'm always grateful when friends who own boats give me freshly caught fish. Even better is when they take me fishing. Louisiana has 41 percent of the nation's wetlands and over seven thousand miles of coastline, and all this water makes fishing an extremely popular pastime. Every year, more than a half-million recreational anglers trek to inland waters and to the Gulf Coast to try their luck, and it's rare that they come home empty-handed.

Fishing is a great activity for kids, and when it wasn't hunting season, my dad, like so many others, used to take us fishing. When we went saltwater fishing, we'd usually rent a "camp," a rustic vacation home, on Grand Isle, which is

Jay crawfishing along the levee near the Atchafalaya Spillway.

fifty-four miles south of New Orleans. Grand Isle is Louisiana's only inhabited barrier island along the state's 397-mile Gulf coastline. The island's normal population is around 1,200, but during the summer it swells to over 20,000, with anglers hoping to catch some of the area's 280 species of fish. Grand Isle is particularly busy at the end of every July, when it hosts its annual International Tarpon Fishing Rodeo, the oldest saltwater fishing contest in the United States.

Today, my typical fishing day in the Gulf Coast's shallow waters and inlets often starts with the purchase of live shrimp for bait. Fishing in a bay or within sight of land, you can expect to catch drum, redfish, flounder, and sheepshead, which used to be considered a trash fish, but which is increasingly appearing on restaurant menus. The prize shallow-saltwater fish is speckled trout, known other places as the spotted seatrout. It's a silvery fish with black dots, and it ranges in size from one to three pounds. I have eaten many, many fried speckled trout in my life, and consider this white flaky fish one of the culinary best.

For deepwater fishing, boats usually go fifteen to thirty miles out to oil rigs, which provide a rich habitat for fish. Bigger boats sail out as far as one hundred miles. From these open waters, anglers can expect to catch amberjack, red snapper, cobia, king mackerel, wahoo, mangrove snapper, ling, and tuna. I have wonderful memories of standing sunburned on an offshore fishing boat and eating a freshly sliced piece of tuna with wasabi.

Even if the fish aren't biting, the crabs usually are. Recreational fishermen catch the Gulf of Mexico's blue crabs three ways, with bait tied to a long heavy string, with a collapsible wire crab net, or with a rectangular chicken-wire trap. Crabs go nuts for raw meat, and fresh chicken necks have always been my preferred bait.

I've also done plenty of freshwater fishing. My family used to make regular pilgrimages to the Toledo Bend Reservoir on the Sabine River between Texas and the northern part of Louisiana. Toledo Bend is the largest artificial lake in the South, and we'd rent cabins and spend our time catching sacalait and bass, and "jerking" the smaller bream and perch out of the water when the cork went under. In Louisiana, bream, as well as catfish, seem to inhabit most decent-sized bodies of fresh water.

At my family's home, I, like many Louisiana youngsters, did my share of recreational crawfishing. In the spring, crawfish seem to crawl out of every ditch and puddle, and catching them with a baited string or even by hand is a snap. When you're boiling for a crowd, like I do now, you need sacks of crawfish, which I buy from farmers, local seafood markets, and grocery stores. But it's those handfuls of crawfish that I caught as a child and boiled in a small saucepan that stick in my memory.

# CHARGRILLED OYSTERS

MAKES 24

½ cup (1 stick) unsalted butter, room temperature

2 tablespoons Jay D's Blanc du Bois wine, or your favorite dry white wine

2 tablespoons grated Parmesan cheese

2 tablespoons minced chives

1 tablespoon minced fresh garlic

2 dozen freshly shucked oysters on the half shell

For serving: crusty French bread slices

**Chargrilled oysters are best prepared with simple butters. If you add a heavy sauce or a mountain of gloopy cheese, the distinctive sea-breeze flavor of the oyster gets lost.**

**1.** In a bowl, blend together the butter, wine, cheese, chives, and garlic. Transfer the mixture to a sheet of parchment paper. Fold one long edge of the parchment over and under the butter. Smooth the butter into a 12-inch-long log. Wrap the log completely with the paper, and refrigerate until firm.

**2.** When ready to cook the oysters, preheat a covered grill to medium-high. Leave oysters in their half-shells and top each with a ½-inch slice (1 tablespoon) of the seasoned butter. Carefully place the oysters on the grill, balancing them on the grates. Close the cover and grill until sauce is bubbling vigorously, about 6–8 minutes. Serve immediately with bread for dipping.

# PAN-FRIED OYSTERS

MAKES 6 SERVINGS

**1.** In a small mixing bowl, beat the eggs with the milk and salt until smooth. In another bowl combine the cornmeal and cracker meal. Pick up an oyster with a fork, dip it into the egg wash, then toss into the dry batter and coat completely. Place the battered oyster on a tray and repeat the process with the rest of the oysters.

**2.** Over the medium-high heat of a propane burner or your stove, heat the lard in a large cast-iron skillet until it is near its smoking point. Place a handful of prepared oysters in the hot lard and fry until golden brown, turning them over once. (Don't overcrowd, or the oil will cool too much.) The cooking time should take about 2 minutes total. Remove the oysters from the skillet and drain on a plate or tray lined with paper towels. Serve while hot and crispy.

4 large eggs

2 tablespoons milk

1 teaspoon kosher salt

1 cup cornmeal

1 cup cracker meal (finely crush up some saltine crackers inside a plastic bag)

1 quart shucked oysters, drained

$\frac{1}{2}$ cup lard

# FRIED CALAMARI WITH SESAME OIL SAUCE

MAKES 6 SERVINGS

2 tablespoons black sesame seeds

1 pound thinly sliced calamari rounds and tentacles

Vegetable oil for frying

2 cups all-purpose flour

2 tablespoons cornstarch

1 teaspoon chipotle chili powder

1 teaspoon smoked paprika

1/2 teaspoon cayenne pepper

1 teaspoon kosher salt, plus more for sprinkling

1 teaspoon freshly ground black pepper

1/4 cup chopped green onion

For serving: Sesame Oil Sauce (recipe follows)

**1.** To toast sesame seeds, preheat a covered grill or your oven to 400°F. While the grill is heating, clean the calamari in cold water and lightly pat dry, leaving some water so dry batter will stick. Set aside. When the grill or your oven is hot, spread the sesame seeds in a skillet and toast 10 minutes. Remove seeds to a small bowl and set aside.

**2.** Heat at least 2 inches oil in a Dutch oven set over a propane burner or your stove to 375°F. In a medium bowl, combine flour, cornstarch, chipotle chili powder, smoked paprika, cayenne, 1 teaspoon salt, and black pepper. Add calamari to the bowl and toss to cover every piece evenly.

**3.** In batches, fry calamari until golden brown, about 2 minutes. Remove to a paper towel-lined bowl and sprinkle with salt.

**4.** To serve, arrange calamari on a platter and sprinkle with toasted sesame seeds and green onion. Serve with Sesame Oil Sauce on the side.

# SESAME OIL SAUCE

MAKES 1 CUP

1/2 cup soy sauce

2 tablespoons sesame oil

1 tablespoon sriracha sauce

1 tablespoon honey

2 teaspoons lime juice

1 teaspoon finely grated fresh ginger

**This is good with any fried seafood.**

Put everything into a glass jar with a cover and shake well. Keeps in the refrigerator 3 days.

# CRAB AU GRATIN

MAKES 4 SERVINGS

1. Preheat a grill or your oven to 375°F. Melt the butter in a 10-inch cast-iron skillet set over the medium-high flame of a propane burner or your stove. Add the onion, celery, green onion, and garlic. Cook, stirring occasionally, until vegetables are soft, 3–5 minutes.

2. While the vegetables cook, in a small bowl vigorously whisk together the evaporated milk and egg yolks. Set aside.

3. Add the flour to the skillet with the vegetables. With heat at medium, make a white roux by stirring mixture constantly about 2 minutes. Do not let roux turn brown.

4. Whisk the milk mixture into the roux mixture, stirring constantly. Stir in the salt, black pepper, and cayenne, and continue stirring until thick, another 3–5 minutes. Remove from heat and fold in half the cheese. Stir until cheese is totally melted and fully incorporated.

5. Gently fold in crab; try not to break apart lumps. Top evenly with the cheese sauce, then sprinkle with the remaining cup of grated cheese. Cover skillet with foil and bake on the preheated grill until bubbly, about 15 minutes. Remove the foil and grill or broil in your oven until the cheese begins to brown, about 5 minutes. Remove from grill and sprinkle with the parsley. Allow to sit 5 minutes before serving.

½ cup (1 stick) unsalted butter

1 medium onion, finely chopped

2 celery ribs, finely chopped

2 tablespoons chopped green onion, white part only

1 tablespoon minced garlic

1 (12-ounce) can evaporated milk

2 large egg yolks, slightly beaten

½ cup all-purpose flour

1 teaspoon kosher salt

1 teaspoon freshly ground black pepper

½ teaspoon cayenne pepper

2 cups finely grated Gruyère cheese, divided

1 pound jumbo lump Gulf crab meat, picked over for shells

1 tablespoon minced fresh parsley

# SPICED SOFT-SHELL CRAB PO'BOY WITH AVOCADO DRESSING

MAKES 2 SANDWICHES

2 large soft-shell crabs, cleaned by removing the eyes, mouth, gills, and the apron (the small flap on the underside)

1 large egg white

1 tablespoon cold water

3 tablespoons rice flour

3 tablespoons cornmeal

¼ cup finely chopped fresh cilantro

2 teaspoons cumin seeds

2 teaspoons ground coriander

½ teaspoon red chili powder, or hot pepper flakes

⅛ teaspoon ground turmeric

Canola oil for frying

1 tablespoon butter

2 brioche buns (6-inch-long or round)

Avocado Dressing (recipe follows)

1 large tomato, sliced

4 romaine lettuce leaves

2 slices red onion

For serving: cornichons and 3 red radishes, sliced

The po'boy sandwich was invented in New Orleans during a 1929 streetcar strike, when restaurateur brothers Clovis and Bennie Martin offered free sandwiches to the out-of-work "poor boys." The Martins used long French loaves, which is traditional, but this sandwich is just as outstanding when made with the brioche buns I use in this recipe. Soft-shell crabs are crabs that have molted their hard shell and are developing a new one, and at this stage, you can eat it shell and all.

**1.** Rinse the cleaned soft-shell crabs and pat dry. Place the egg white in a medium bowl and whisk with the water. Place rice flour in a small shallow plate, and place cornmeal in a separate shallow plate. Divide the cilantro, cumin, coriander, chili powder, and turmeric evenly between the flour and cornmeal and stir well.

**2.** Dip a crab into the egg white mixture, then coat both sides with the seasoned rice flour. Place the crab into the egg white again, then coat with the seasoned cornmeal. Repeat with second crab.

**3.** Over medium-high heat of a propane burner or your stove, heat 2 inches oil in a deep frying pan or wok. Place the crabs into the hot oil and fry on one side 3 minutes. Flip the crabs and cook until golden brown, another 3 minutes. (To be sure oil stays hot, cook no more than 2 at a time.) Drain fried crabs on paper towels.

**4.** Place butter in a large cast-iron skillet and melt over medium-high heat. Spread the melting butter to coat pan evenly. Place the buns, open side down, onto the pan and grill for 1 minute. Flip the buns and grill the outside for another 1 minute. Remove hot buns to 2 plates.

**5.** Coat the insides of both buns with Avocado Dressing. Assemble sandwiches in this order: fried crab, tomato slices, lettuce leaves, and onion. Garnish with cornichons and radish slices.

# AVOCADO DRESSING

MAKES ½ CUP

**Great on sandwiches, and equally good on a hefty iceberg-lettuce salad.**

Mash the avocado in a bowl. Add remaining ingredients and stir together until creamy. Use the same day.

½ of a medium, ripe avocado

Juice of ½ large lemon

1 teaspoon extra virgin olive oil

¼ teaspoon salt

¼ teaspoon ground black pepper

# BARBECUED SHRIMP

MAKES 2 SERVINGS

¼ cup Jay D's Louisiana Barbecue Sauce (purchased or recipe page 186, or your favorite commercial brand)

¼ cup canola oil

¼ cup minced garlic

1 tablespoon freshly ground black pepper

1 tablespoon Louisiana-style hot sauce

½ teaspoon cayenne pepper

1 pound large head-on shrimp, unpeeled

1 loaf French bread

½ cup Barbecue Butter for Seafood, divided (recipe follows)

½ cup heavy whipping cream

1 tablespoon Jay D's Spicy & Sweet Barbecue Rub (purchased or recipe page 183, or your favorite commercial brand)

For serving: ¼ cup chopped green onion

Louisiana's traditional barbecued shrimp dish is cooked in a skillet on the stove, so it isn't barbecued at all. Since I like to cook mine on a grill, my recipe is the exception.

**1.** To marinate the shrimp, in a gallon resealable food-safe plastic bag, combine barbecue sauce, canola oil, garlic, black pepper, hot sauce, and cayenne. Squish everything around until it's combined. Add shrimp, seal the bag, and refrigerate 4 hours.

**2.** When you're ready to cook, heat a grill to medium-high or an indoor oven to 375°F. Cut the French bread into ½-inch crostini, and spread 1 side of each slice with 1 teaspoon of the Barbecue Butter. Grill, or place the crostini on a sheet pan and bake until golden brown, 5–7 minutes. Set aside.

**3.** Heat a large cast-iron skillet set on the hot grill or over medium-high stove heat. Drain the shrimp and cook on one side 3 minutes. Flip the shrimp and add the cream. Reduce cream by half. Add the remaining Barbecue Butter and the barbecue rub. Cook until the sauce is slightly thick and creamy. Plate the shrimp and the sauce in large shallow bowls, and garnish with green onion and crostini. Serve immediately.

# BARBECUE BUTTER FOR SEAFOOD

MAKES ABOUT 2 CUPS

**Try this savory butter on any grilled or sautéed seafood.**

**1.** Heat a skillet over medium propane or stove heat and melt 2 tablespoons of the butter. Add the garlic, rosemary, and oregano, and cook until the garlic is soft, about 2 minutes.

**2.** Add the barbecue sauce and cook 2 more minutes. Pour the contents of the skillet into the bowl of a standing mixer and allow it to cool. Once cool, add the remaining butter and black pepper. Whip on medium mixer speed until double in size, 4–5 minutes. Use immediately or refrigerate, tightly covered, up to 1 week.

1 cup (2 sticks) unsalted butter, room temperature, divided

¼ cup minced garlic

1 tablespoon minced fresh rosemary

1 tablespoon minced fresh oregano

¼ cup Jay D's Louisiana Barbecue Sauce, (purchased or recipe page 186, or your favorite commercial brand)

1 teaspoon freshly ground black pepper

**Barbecued shrimp.**

# BLACKENED SHRIMP WITH GRITS

MAKES 4 ENTRÉE SERVINGS

2 cups chicken stock

2 cups whole milk

Kosher salt and ground black pepper to taste

1 cup stone-ground yellow grits

4 tablespoons (1/2 stick) unsalted butter

1 1/2 pounds fresh shrimp, peeled and deveined

3 tablespoons Jay D's Spicy & Sweet Barbecue Rub (purchased or recipe page 183, or your favorite commercial brand)

2 tablespoons canola oil

1/2 bunch green onions, chopped

**1.** In a large saucepan set over a propane burner or your stove, bring to a boil the stock, milk, 1/4 teaspoon salt, and pepper to taste. Whisk in the grits well and lower to a simmer. Cover the pot and cook, stirring occasionally, until smooth and creamy, about 30 minutes. Stir in the butter and additional salt and pepper. Remove grits from heat and leave covered.

**2.** Sprinkle the shrimp with the barbecue rub. In a large cast-iron skillet, heat the oil over medium-high heat. Working in batches, cook the shrimp until they're charred on the outside and opaque on the inside, about 2 minutes per side.

**3.** Divide the hot grits among 4 plates and top with the shrimp. Sprinkle with the green onion and serve immediately.

# CRUCIFEROUS CRUNCH SHRIMP, SWEET POTATO, AND QUINOA SALAD

MAKES 4 SERVINGS

**1.** Preheat a covered grill or your oven to 400°F. Toss sweet potatoes with 1 tablespoon olive oil and salt and pepper to taste. Roast in a large cast-iron skillet over covered indirect grill heat or in the oven until tender, about 30–45 minutes.

**2.** In a medium saucepan, bring water to a boil over a propane burner or your stove and stir in quinoa. Cover and simmer 15 minutes. Turn heat off and keep covered 5 minutes.

**3.** Meanwhile, season shrimp with avocado oil and barbecue rub. Place a large sauté pan over the medium heat of a propane burner or your stove. Add remaining tablespoon olive oil, then add shrimp. Sauté until shrimp are translucent, about 3–5 minutes. Set aside.

**4.** Place raw vegetables in a large bowl and add sweet potatoes and quinoa. Mix molasses mustard and jalapeño olive oil together and drizzle over everything in the bowl. Toss and divide among 4 large plates. Top with the shrimp and serve immediately.

1 large (1-pound) sweet potato, peeled and cubed into 1-inch squares

2 tablespoons olive oil, divided

Salt and ground black pepper

2 cups water

1 cup tricolored quinoa

1 pound raw large shrimp, peeled and deveined

1 tablespoon avocado oil

2 tablespoons Jay D's Spicy & Sweet Barbecue Rub (purchased or recipe page 183, or your favorite commercial brand)

1½ cups raw, shredded cruciferous vegetable mixture (kale, Brussels sprouts, cabbage, bok choy, watercress, etc.)

¼ cup Jay D's Louisiana Molasses Mustard, (purchased or recipe page 184)

2 tablespoons jalapeño extra virgin olive oil

# MOLASSES MUSTARD-FRIED CATFISH

MAKES 4 SERVINGS

Peanut, canola, or other mild-flavored oil for frying

1 cup Jay D's Louisiana Molasses Mustard (recipe page 184, or plain yellow mustard)

1 cup whole milk

4 tablespoons Louisiana-style hot sauce

3 cups commercial fish-fry coating mix or seasoned cornmeal

2 tablespoons Jay D's Spicy & Sweet Barbecue Rub (purchased or recipe page 183, or your favorite commercial brand)

1 teaspoon kosher salt

1 pound catfish fillets, sliced into small strips

For serving: Creole Tartar Sauce (recipe follows)

Using molasses mustard in this recipe adds a hint of sweetness. If you'd prefer a strictly savory catfish crust, use plain prepared yellow mustard.

**1.** In a large Dutch oven or deep fryer set over a propane burner or your stove, pour oil to a depth of four inches. Heat over a medium flame until oil reaches 350° on a deep-fry thermometer.

**2.** While oil is heating, pour the mustard, milk, and hot sauce into a shallow dish or aluminum pan and mix well. In another shallow dish, stir together fish-fry, barbecue rub, and salt. Coat each fish fillet in the mustard, then dredge in cornmeal mixture.

**3.** Fry fillets in batches in hot oil until golden brown and cooked through, about 6 to 8 minutes. Drain on paper towels. Serve hot with Creole Tartar Sauce for dipping.

# CREOLE TARTAR SAUCE

MAKES ¾ CUP

This flavor-packed sauce goes with anything fried. It's also good on a sandwich instead of plain mayonnaise.

Put all ingredients into a food processor and pulse until smooth. Refrigerate at least 2 hours for flavors to combine. Keeps in the refrigerator 1 week.

½ cup mayonnaise

2 tablespoons minced pickled okra

1 tablespoon fresh-squeezed lemon juice

1 tablespoon Creole mustard

1 tablespoon Worcestershire sauce

1 teaspoon minced garlic

¼ teaspoon cayenne pepper

Molasses mustard–fried catfish.

# WHOLE GRILLED RED SNAPPER

MAKES 4 SERVINGS

Zest and juice of 1 lemon

12 sprigs fresh oregano, divided

6 cloves peeled garlic, divided

1 teaspoon kosher salt

1 teaspoon ground black pepper

½ teaspoon crushed red pepper

2 tablespoons pecan oil or grapeseed oil, plus additional for oiling grill

1 whole (4- to 6-pound) red snapper, scaled, gills removed, gutted, rinsed, and patted dry

For serving: 1 lemon, sliced thin into whole moons

**1.** In the bowl of a food processor, combine the zest and juice of 1 lemon, leaves from 6 sprigs oregano, 2 cloves garlic, salt, black pepper, and red pepper. Pulse to combine. With motor running, slowly pour in pecan oil, and pulse until combined. Set aside.

**2.** Score snapper on both sides with parallel slices two inches apart between the fins and the tail, cutting down to the bone. Fill the fish's cavity with lemon slices, remaining 6 oregano sprigs, and remaining 4 cloves garlic.

**3.** Rub herb mixture onto the snapper on both sides, being careful of the dorsal fin, which can be sharp. Cover and refrigerate 1 to 2 hours.

**4.** Rub a grill rack with pecan oil. Prepare grill for direct and indirect grilling, and heat to medium-high (350°F to 400°F). Place snapper over direct heat, and cook until it begins to char, 2 to 3 minutes per side. Carefully move snapper to indirect heat, and cover grill. Cook until flaky throughout, 5 to 7 minutes more, depending on the size of the fish and temperature of the grill. Carefully transfer snapper to a serving platter, garnish with lemon slices, and serve immediately.

# SIMPLE SALMON

**Even though salmon is not native to Louisiana, this supermarket favorite is often my go-to meal when I'm in a rush. For that reason I merely use mustard and a barbecue rub to season this dish.**

Preheat a grill to medium heat, or your oven to 400°F. Mix the molasses mustard and barbecue rub together and set aside. Pat salmon filets dry. Brush the hot grill with olive oil. For the oven, oil a foil-lined sheet pan. Spoon mustard mixture on the tops of the fish filets and spread evenly. Grill or bake, skin side up, for 6 minutes. Flip over and continue grilling until flaky, about 6–7 minutes more. Serve immediately.

¼ cup Jay D's Louisiana Molasses Mustard (purchased or recipe page 184)

1 tablespoon Jay D's Spicy & Sweet Barbecue Rub (purchased or recipe page 183, or your favorite commercial brand)

4 (6- to 8-ounce) salmon filets

Olive oil for brushing the grill or baking pan

# BOILED CRAWFISH

MAKES 8 SERVINGS

1 sack (around 35 pounds) live
Louisiana crawfish

1 cup table salt for soaking crawfish

Lots of water

4 pounds dry Cajun seafood boil
seasoning (from specialty stores
or online; I prefer Slap Ya Mama
brand)

1 cup cayenne pepper

1 cup liquid crab boil seasoning
(from specialty stores or online)

1 cup kosher salt

5 pounds oranges, halved

3 pounds lemons, halved

5 pounds yellow onions, halved

10 whole heads garlic

5 pounds small red potatoes,
purchased in mesh bags, or bag
your own

5 pounds corn on the cob, shucked

3 pounds fresh button mushrooms

**It's always best to taste the crawfish throughout the final soaking
process. You want the seasoning to soak in, but you don't want to
overcook the crawfish, which will make them too hard to peel.**

**1.** Pour live crawfish into a large ice chest or wash tub. Sprinkle with table
salt. Add enough water to cover and let crawfish soak 10 minutes. Drain the
water.

**2.** Fill an 80-quart crawfish pot ½ full with water and add seasonings, citrus,
onions, and garlic. Over an outdoor propane burner, bring to a rolling boil.
Add the potatoes in their bags. Reduce heat to medium-low. Boil until potatoes are fork-tender, about 20 minutes. Remove potatoes and set aside.

**3.** Bring water back to a rolling boil. Add crawfish, corn, and mushrooms.
If crawfish are soft (beginning of season), boil for 3 minutes and soak for 17.
If you have late-season crawfish that are hard, boil longer and soak less. Boiling and soaking time should always equal 20 minutes. Taste tails throughout
the soaking process for doneness. Tail meat should remove easily without
breaking.

**4.** To serve, drain the cooked crawfish. Spread newspaper on an outdoor
table, and dump crawfish and vegetables on the top. Serve with lots of paper
towels and cold beer.

# CRAWFISH ROLLS

MAKES 4 SERVINGS

**If you have leftover crawfish from a crawfish boil, clean the tails and whip up these simple, flavorful sandwiches.**

1. Preheat a grill to medium, or your oven to 350°F. Combine butter and barbecue sauce and set aside.

2. In a mixing bowl, combine crawfish, aioli, green onion, celery, and Creole seasoning. Set aside.

3. Spread 1 tablespoon of the barbecue-sauce butter all over the outsides of each roll. Toast the rolls on the grill or in the oven until heated through, 3–4 minutes. Split each roll, fill with crawfish mixture, and serve immediately.

¼ cup (½ stick) soft butter

2 tablespoons Jay D's Louisiana Barbecue Sauce (recipe page 186 or your favorite commercial brand)

1 pound peeled and cooked crawfish tails from a crawfish boil

½ cup Barbecue Aioli (recipe page 185)

¼ cup chopped green onion

¼ cup diced celery

1 teaspoon Creole seasoning (purchased or recipe page 182)

4 soft buttery rolls

# CRAWFISH BOUDIN

MAKES 8 SERVINGS

2 pounds crawfish tails

1½ teaspoons salt

½ teaspoon cayenne pepper

¼ teaspoon freshly ground white pepper

2 tablespoons canola oil

1 cup finely diced onion

½ cup finely diced green bell peppers

½ cup finely diced celery

¼ teaspoon minced garlic

⅓ cup minced green onion, green parts only

3 cups cooked rice (recipe page 166)

2 tablespoons finely chopped parsley

8 ounces cleaned and prepared hog casings

**Seafood boudin is becoming more and more popular. Make the boudin and stuff the casings a day ahead. When you're ready to serve, all you have to do is heat it in water.**

**1.** Mix the crawfish tails with salt, cayenne, and white pepper and set aside.

**2.** Heat a large sauté pan over the medium-high heat of a propane burner or stove and add canola oil. Sauté the onion, bell peppers, celery, and garlic until soft, about 5 minutes. Add seasoned crawfish and green onion, and cook on medium heat for 15 minutes.

**3.** Remove from heat and fold in rice and parsley. While mixture is still hot, use a sausage stuffer to stuff casings, twisting into 4-inch links.

**4.** To cook, lay links in a large pan, cover with tap water, and heat water to just below simmering. Gently cook until heated through, about 15–20 minutes. Drain and serve.

**Special equipment:** A sausage stuffer

# CRAWFISH FRICASSEE

MAKES 4 SERVINGS

A Louisiana fricassee is a delicately seasoned stew made with a light-colored roux. Cajuns will fricassee just about any edible critter. I'm partial to this crawfish recipe.

**1.** Set a large saucepan over the medium-high heat of a propane burner or stove and melt the butter with the olive oil. Add flour and whisk constantly to create a blonde roux. Should take 4 to 5 minutes.

**2.** Add the onion, carrot, celery, tomato, mushrooms, and garlic and cook over medium heat 5 minutes. Stir in the chicken stock, wine, bay leaves, and thyme. Season with a little salt and white pepper, then simmer, uncovered, 20 minutes.

**3.** Add the crawfish tails and cook 5 minutes. Check seasoning and add salt and white pepper to taste. Serve over hot rice.

4 tablespoons unsalted butter

1 tablespoon extra virgin olive oil

¼ cup all-purpose flour

1 cup finely diced yellow onion

½ cup finely diced carrot

½ cup finely diced celery

½ cup peeled, seeded, and coarsely chopped tomato

4 ounces fresh mushrooms, trimmed and quartered

1 tablespoon minced garlic

1 quart chicken stock

⅔ cup Jay D's Blanc du Bois wine, or your favorite dry white wine

2 bay leaves

2 sprigs fresh thyme

Kosher salt to taste

White pepper to taste

2 pounds cleaned crawfish tails

For serving: hot cooked rice (recipe page 166)

# CRAWFISH ÉTOUFFÉE

MAKES 4 SERVINGS

½ cup (1 stick) unsalted butter

½ cup all-purpose flour

3 stalks celery, minced

1 large onion, minced

1 large bell pepper, any color, seeded and minced

1 tablespoon minced garlic

2 cups seafood or clam broth

¼ cup chopped fresh parsley, divided

3 tablespoons tomato paste

1 teaspoon chopped fresh thyme, or ½ teaspoon dried

2 dried bay leaves

¼ teaspoon liquid crab boil seasoning (found in specialty stores or online), optional

Salt, freshly ground black pepper, and cayenne pepper to taste

1 pound cleaned crawfish tails

For serving: hot cooked rice (recipe page 166) and chopped green onion

Étouffée is a French word that literally means "smothered." In Cajun and Creole cooking, it's a hefty stew-like dish of shellfish served over rice, and it's usually seasoned with a heavy dose of pepper. Liquid crab boil is a potent commercial blend of spices and pepper that we use mostly to season boiled crab, shrimp, and crawfish. A small amount of crab boil in any kind of seafood gravy adds a mountain of flavor.

**1.** Melt the butter in a Dutch oven set over the medium-high heat of a propane burner or your stove. Whisk in flour and stir constantly until you have a roux the color of a paper grocery bag, about 10 minutes. Roux should be an even color, without any black specks.

**2.** Stir in celery, onion, bell pepper, and garlic. Cook and stir 5 minutes. Add broth and bring to a simmer. Stir in 3 tablespoons parsley, tomato paste, thyme, bay leaves, crab boil, and seasonings. Bring to a fast simmer and cook until vegetables are tender and sauce has thickened, about 10 minutes.

**3.** Add crawfish tails, bring to a simmer, and cook 10 minutes. Remove and discard bay leaves. Serve étouffée over rice garnished with remaining tablespoon parsley and green onion.

# POULTRY & GAME BIRDS

There's a suburban and inner-city trend of raising chickens in backyards. Most people I know with chickens keep them to collect fresh eggs. Some do butcher their broods for their incomparable tasting meat, but that's not something I hear about often. From what I've been told, just fifty years ago it was common to drive up to a house, even in the middle of a town, and find domestic birds pecking in the yard. Aside from chickens, that could include guinea hens, turkeys, ducks, and geese, and most of those birds ended up in a pot.

Although people hardly raise the so-called uncommon birds anymore, even in the country, it is increasingly easy to find different varieties of locally raised poultry in farmers' markets. On a large commercial scale, our chicken farmers annually produce almost one billion pounds of broilers. The growing poultry industry is the state's largest animal agricultural business, with a $1.24 billion contribution to the economy.

Like most cooks, when it comes to preparing poultry, chicken is the bird I turn to most. But I also often grill turkey and domestic duck. If I'm in the mood to make something special and I have wild ducks or geese in the freezer, they definitely get the nod for the entrée.

Luckily for us hunters, the Gulf of Mexico is the end of the line for many of the birds that follow the Mississippi flyway. This migratory route begins in breeding grounds in western Canada, and in what is known as the United States' Prairie Pothole Region, the states of North and South Dakota, Iowa, Minnesota, and Montana. The route generally follows the 2,300-mile-long Mississippi River. The conservation organization Ducks Unlimited estimates that half of the game birds flapping south along the flyway end up in Louisiana.

Of the millions of ducks that come here every winter, some of the more common are pintails, gadwalls, mallards, wigeon, and teal. Goose varieties include specklebellies, white-fronted, and snow geese. Ducks and geese not only like our temperate climate, but they also gorge on the smorgasbord of grasses found in Louisiana's soupy marshes and rice fields.

Bird hunting is one of my favorite sports. At some point during the winter hunting season, you're likely to find me carrying my trusty 12-gauge shotgun as I sneak toward a hiding place in a rice field. To lure in a skeptical duck, a hunter must blend into the surroundings, so I'll be dressed in my full hunter's camouflage. Although many hunters hole up in a fancy building hidden in brush, I typically crouch into a ground blind, a dirt dugout surrounded by tall grass.

The prizes I bring home from duck hunts make for some of the most spectacular meals I've produced. Wild duck meat is all dark. If prepared properly, baked duck is moist and tender, and it doesn't have a gamey taste. My favorite way of cooking duck is to sear the breasts medium rare. Wild goose, which is also dark, is a little tough, so I usually cook it in a gumbo that, when combined with smoked sausage, is incomparable.

Winter is also the time for hunting small game birds. I shot my first quail when I was around ten or eleven, with a 16-gauge shotgun. We were in Texas, where there's an abundance of bobwhites and the larger blue-feathered or "blue" quail. That day I brought home a sizable contribution to dinner. Another first that involves quail is my first cooking experience with alcohol. Back at a high school pool party, I brought along a bunch of quail I'd shot, and I marinated them in Jack Daniel's that I found in my friend's parents' bar, wrapped them in bacon, and grilled them. Soon I was the most popular guy there.

Today, if my freezer's empty and I crave grilled quail, I run to the nearest independent grocer or to the farmers' market for farm-raised quail. A commercial quail is not as large or as fully flavored as wild quail, but it's an excellent substitute. Wild quail used to be much more plentiful in Texas and Louisiana. (I once heard a story about how quail used to run wild down the streets of New Orleans.) Unfortunately, loss of habitat is diminishing their numbers. Both states are conducting research into the problem, and hopefully with good conservation and hunting practices, large numbers of quail will once again be peeping in our fields.

Another bird I love hunting is dove. It's sort of a tradition in Louisiana to hunt doves on opening day, and doing so is always a thrill. What we see here mostly are migrating mourning doves. This prolific breeder is attracted to the southwest part of the state, with its fields of soybeans and rice, and abundant water and trees where doves can roost. It takes good shooting to bag these dipping and diving targets, and just trying to knock them down greatly sharpens shotgun skills.

Like wild duck and geese, wild doves have dark-meat breasts. If not cooked properly, doves can be dry, but that problem is easily remedied with a mari-

**Wings going onto the grill.**

nade. One of my favorite dove recipes is to breast out a dove and wrap it with bacon and throw it on the grill. To me, that's a perfect appetizer.

It's been a while, but another bird I've hunted is wild turkey. The eastern wild turkey is Louisiana's largest native game bird, and it is most prevalent in the woods of central and north Louisiana. With dwindling populations, the Louisiana turkey hunting season lasts only about a month, in the spring. Hunters are limited to two gobblers, or toms (males) per season, one per day. A gobbler is easy to identify, with large red wattles under its beak. Wild turkey is flavorful, but it is tough. Marinade always helps, or you can do like I do, smoke it and cook it in gumbo. Any game bird seems to turn out good that way.

# BLACKENED PEACH AND CHICKEN SALAD

MAKES 2 SERVINGS

2 boneless, skinless chicken breasts

Canola oil

Kosher salt

Jay D's Spicy & Sweet Barbecue Rub (purchased or recipe page 183, or your favorite commercial brand)

4 whole ripe peaches, peeled and pitted

Olive oil

4 cups salad greens (iceberg, romaine, leaf lettuce, or spinach)

¼ cup Jay D's Louisiana Molasses Mustard (purchased or recipe page 184)

6 cherry tomatoes, halved

¼ cup crumbled feta cheese

**I make this entrée salad throughout the local summer peach season, which can extend from April through mid-August.**

**1.** Preheat a covered grill or your oven to 350°F. Coat chicken breasts on both sides with canola oil, a dash of salt, and barbecue rub. Over a propane burner or your stove, heat a cast-iron skillet over medium-high heat and add chicken. Cook until the first side starts to blacken, about 1 minute. Turn and repeat. Move chicken and skillet to covered grill or oven and cook until the middle of the meat is cooked all the way through, to 165°F.

**2.** Prepare an outdoor or indoor grill for high heat. Cut the peaches into fourths and lightly coat them with olive oil. Place peaches on the grill and cook until charred, about 1 minute each side. Remove to a bowl.

**3.** In a large bowl, toss salad greens with Molasses Mustard. Divide between 2 cold plates. Top with cherry tomato halves and feta cheese. Cut chicken into ½-inch strips and place on top of lettuce. Top that with grilled peaches and serve immediately.

# BARBECUED CHICKEN QUESADILLAS

**MAKES 4 SERVINGS**

**1.** Spread ¼ cup chicken on half a side of each tortilla. Top chicken with equal amounts of sliced onion, cheese, and barbecue sauce. Fold tortilla in half.

**2.** Heat a large, heavy skillet over high grill or stove heat. Add enough oil to coat the bottom of the pan. Lower the heat to medium. Add the quesadillas to the skillet and cook until golden brown on both sides, about 3 minutes per side. Slice into 4 pieces, and garnish with sliced green onion. Drizzle with Barbecue Aioli.

1 cup cooked, shredded chicken

4 (12-inch) flour tortillas (purchased or recipe page 175)

1 red onion, thinly sliced

12 ounces Monterey Jack cheese, shredded

½ cup Jay D's Louisiana Barbecue Sauce (purchased or recipe page 186, or your favorite commercial brand)

Olive oil

For serving: ½ cup sliced green onion and Barbecue Aioli (recipe page 185)

# CHICKEN BISCUITS WITH MOLASSES MUSTARD BUTTER

MAKES 6 SERVINGS

1 recipe for Biscuits using a 3½-inch biscuit cutter (recipe follows)

Canola oil for frying

¾ cup all-purpose flour

1 teaspoon kosher salt

1 teaspoon ground black pepper

1 large egg

1 tablespoon water

3 chicken breast halves, each cut in half and flattened

1 stick unsalted butter, at room temperature

⅓ cup Jay D's Louisiana Molasses Mustard (or recipe page 184)

**1.** Prepare the biscuits. As soon as they're out of the oven, start the chicken.

**2.** For the chicken, heat 2 inches canola oil to 350°F in a Dutch oven set over a propane burner or your stove. Combine flour, salt, and pepper in a shallow bowl or plate. In another shallow bowl, whisk together the egg and water. Dredge chicken in seasoned flour, place in egg wash, then dredge again through flour. Fry chicken until golden brown, about 4–5 minutes total.

**3.** To make molasses butter, mix together the butter and molasses mustard. Slice biscuits open and slather the insides with molasses mustard butter. Place fried chicken breasts between biscuit halves and serve immediately.

# BISCUITS

**Adapted from a recipe by my friend and former Hogs for the Cause barbecue contest teammate, "King Biscuit," Chef Alex Hamman. This is an amazingly good all-purpose biscuit, with lots of flakes and a soft inside texture. It's the recipe I usually use.**

2 cups bread flour

2 cups cake flour

2 tablespoons baking powder

2 teaspoons kosher salt

2 teaspoons sugar

12 tablespoons (1½ sticks)
cold unsalted butter, cubed

1½ cups cold buttermilk

**1.** Preheat an outdoor covered grill to 400°F for indirect cooking, or your kitchen oven to 375°F. If using a grill, place a metal baking sheet on the grates over the indirect heat. In a medium mixing bowl, combine bread flour, cake flour, baking powder, salt, and sugar. Use a pastry blender or your hands to cut in the butter until it's the size of peas. Add buttermilk and mix with your hands until shaggy. Cover with plastic wrap and let rest 20 minutes.

**2.** Knead dough lightly and roll out on a floured surface. Fold once to create layers, then roll again to ¾- to 1-inch thick and cut into circles. For optimal rise, when cutting out biscuits, do not twist cutter, just simply press down and lift cutter back up.

**3.** If cooking on the grill, place biscuits ½ inch apart in a large, greased cast-iron skillet. Place the skillet of biscuits on the baking sheet you've been heating on the grill. Do not cover the biscuits, but close the grill. In the oven, place biscuits on a greased baking sheet ½ inch apart. Bake until golden brown, about 20–25 minutes for large biscuits and 15–20 minutes for small ones.

# BRAISED CHICKEN FEET

MAKES 8 SERVINGS

2 pounds chicken feet

Kosher salt

Water for boiling

1 cup green onion tops, in 1-inch pieces, plus additional for garnish

½ cup sake

⅓ cup chicken stock

⅓ cup soy sauce

3 tablespoons light brown sugar

2 tablespoons oyster sauce

2 tablespoons hoisin sauce

3 cloves garlic, peeled and sliced

1 tablespoon peeled and minced fresh ginger

1 teaspoon crushed hot chili pepper

2 star anise buds

¼ teaspoon ground cinnamon

For serving: 2 tablespoons fresh cilantro and 1 tablespoon toasted sesame seeds

**My more adventurous friends and customers love this Asian-inspired dish. It takes some work to gnaw the tiny pieces of meat off the bone, but each flavor-packed morsel is worth the effort.**

**1.** Rub chicken feet with salt and let sit 15 minutes. Rinse feet in cold water. Bring a large pot of water and 1 tablespoon salt to a rapid boil. Place feet into pot and blanch 5 minutes. Remove feet from pot and drain well. Rub off as much of the top skin as possible and clip off the toenails.

**2.** When ready to cook, place a large sauté pan over high propane burner or stove heat. Add the chicken feet and dry-sear to lightly brown. Add the remaining ingredients and bring to a simmer. Cook, covered, for 10 minutes. Uncover and simmer until pan is almost dry, tossing frequently to coat the feet as the sauce reduces and thickens.

**3.** To serve, arrange feet on a large serving platter and garnish with onion tops, cilantro, and sesame seeds.

# QUICK BARBECUED CHICKEN PIZZA

MAKES 1 (12-INCH) PIZZA

**1.** Prepare a grill for medium-high heat or preheat your kitchen oven to 450°. Preheat a pizza stone. If you're cooking on an outdoor grill, generously flour a large cookie sheet. If you're cooking in a regular oven, generously grease that cookie sheet. Unroll the pizza dough on the cookie sheet and use your fingers to make a 15×10-inch rectangle with a slightly raised lip around the edges.

**2.** Spread ²/₃ cup barbecue sauce over the crust. In a bowl, toss the chicken with the remaining 2 tablespoons barbecue sauce. Top the pie with the chicken, cheese, and red onion. Slide pizza onto heated stone and close the cover. (Or place cookie sheet with pizza in the oven.) Bake until the cheese melts and the crust is golden, 8–10 minutes. Remove from grill or oven and top with green onion. Slice and serve immediately.

1 can store-bought pizza crust

Flour or oil for preparing the cookie sheet

²/₃ cup, plus 2 tablespoons, Jay D's Louisiana Barbecue Sauce (purchased or recipe page 186, or your favorite commercial brand)

1½ cups shredded cooked chicken (I use leftovers or buy one already cooked)

1½ cups Monterey Jack cheese

1 small red onion, thinly sliced

For serving: ¼ cup sliced green onion

# SPICY AND SWEET CASSOULET WITH BLACKENED CHICKEN

MAKES 6 SERVINGS (BEGIN A DAY AHEAD)

1 pound dried navy beans

Water

2 tablespoons canola oil, divided

1 pound smoked andouille sausage, sliced

1 large onion, finely diced

2 stalks celery, chopped

1 large carrot, cut on the bias a half-inch thick

1 clove garlic, minced

1 quart chicken stock

4 tablespoons Jay D's Spicy & Sweet Barbecue Rub (purchased or recipe page 183), or 4 tablespoons Creole seasoning (purchased or recipe page 182) mixed with 2 teaspoons brown sugar, divided

4 sprigs fresh thyme

2 bay leaves

Salt and ground black pepper to taste

4 boneless, skinless chicken breasts

**1.** Put dried beans in a large bowl and cover by 2 inches water. Allow beans to soak at room temperature overnight. The next day, drain, discard liquid, and set beans aside.

**2.** In a Dutch oven or cast-iron pot set over a propane burner or your stove, heat 1 tablespoon canola oil over medium-high heat and brown sausage well on both sides. Transfer to a small bowl, leaving any accumulated oil in the pan. In the same pan, sauté onion, celery, carrot, and garlic until soft, about 10 minutes.

**3.** Add stock, 2 tablespoons barbecue rub, thyme, bay leaves, sausage, and beans and bring to a boil. Turn down to a simmer, cover, and cook until beans are tender, about 2 hours. Stir every once in a while. Check for seasoning and add more salt and pepper if you think you need it. Set beans aside while preparing chicken.

**4.** To blacken the chicken, place a cast-iron skillet over the medium-high heat of a grill or your stove burner. Season chicken liberally with the remaining barbecue rub. Place remaining tablespoon canola oil into hot skillet, then add chicken (you want it hot enough to sizzle). Cover the grill or skillet and cook 4 minutes on each side. Move skillet to indirect heat or to a 350°F oven. Covered, let it cook until the internal temperature of the chicken reaches 165°F, about 10 minutes.

**5.** While chicken is cooking, reheat beans. Remove cooked chicken from the grill, slice, and serve over individual bowls of warm cassoulet.

# SPICY AND SWEET BUTTER FRIED WINGS

MAKES 2 SERVINGS

If you're a fan of buttered popcorn, you'll like the flavor of these slightly spicy chicken wings.

**1.** Melt butter in a saucepan and stir in the barbecue rub and hot sauce. Set aside.

**2.** Over a propane burner or on your stove, heat 2 inches oil to 350°F in a deep fryer or large Dutch oven. Sprinkle the wings well with salt and pepper and fry until golden brown, 8–10 minutes. Drain wings and toss in a bowl with the butter mixture, making sure every bit of the chicken is coated thoroughly. Serve immediately.

½ cup (1 stick) unsalted butter, softened

2 teaspoons Jay D's Spicy & Sweet Barbecue Rub (purchased or recipe page 183, or your favorite commercial brand)

2 teaspoons Louisiana-style hot sauce, such as Slap Ya Mama Cajun Pepper Sauce

Vegetable oil for frying

1 pound chicken wings

Salt and ground black pepper to taste

# CHICKEN AND DUMPLINGS

MAKES 6 SERVINGS

1 tablespoon canola oil

6 chicken thighs, bone in, skin on

Salt and pepper to taste

3 stalks celery, chopped

3 carrots, chopped

1 medium onion, chopped

5 cloves garlic, minced

2 tablespoons fresh thyme

8 cups chicken broth

¼ cup cornstarch

¼ cup water

For serving: hot cooked rice (recipe page 166)

Dumplings:

2 cups all-purpose flour

1 tablespoon baking powder

½ teaspoon baking soda

¼ teaspoon salt

¼ teaspoon ground black pepper

¾ cup buttermilk

6 tablespoons (¾ stick) unsalted butter, melted

**In south Louisiana we make our dumplings with a batter, not rolled dough. We drop them in the boiling stew with a spoon, and they turn out like savory balls of fluffy bread.**

**1.** To make the chicken stew, heat the oil in a large cast-iron pot or Dutch oven over the medium-high heat of a propane burner or your stove. Season the chicken with salt and pepper. Brown in batches, 4 to 6 minutes per side. Transfer to a plate and leave drippings in the pot.

**2.** Add the celery, carrots, onion, garlic, and thyme to the drippings and cook, stirring, until the vegetables begin to soften, 5 to 7 minutes. Add chicken and chicken broth. Bring to a simmer, and cook, uncovered, until the chicken is cooked through, 25 to 30 minutes. Remove the chicken. When cool enough to handle, shred the meat and return it back to the pot. Discard the bones and skin.

**3.** Whisk the cornstarch and water together slowly, then whisk the slurry into the pot. Simmer until slightly thickened, 8 to 10 minutes.

**4.** To make dumplings, in a medium bowl, whisk together flour, baking powder, baking soda, and salt and pepper. Whisk in buttermilk and melted butter. Reduce the heat under the chicken stew to a bare simmer and drop in blobs of the dumpling mixture from a teaspoon. You should have about 16 dumplings. Simmer, covered, until the dumplings are firm, 12 to 15 minutes. Serve stew and dumplings over hot rice.

# BARBECUED BUTTER TURKEY BREAST

**MAKES 6 SERVINGS (BEGIN A DAY AHEAD)**

**1.** Place turkey in a large bowl or plastic food-safe bag and cover with cooled brine. Cover tightly and let sit in the refrigerator overnight.

**2.** Prepare one side of a covered grill to medium heat, or preheat your oven to 325°F. Remove turkey from brine and pat dry with paper towels. Sprinkle turkey all over with ¼ cup of the barbecue rub. Make the barbecue butter by melting the butter and combining it with the remaining ½ cup barbecue rub.

**3.** Place turkey skin-side-up over indirect grill heat, or on a rack in a roasting pan for oven baking. Roast, uncovered, until the skin is golden brown and an instant-read thermometer registers 165°F when inserted into the meatiest area. Baste with butter mixture every 15 minutes. If the skin starts to over-brown, cover loosely with aluminum foil. Should take between 1½-2 hours.

**4.** Once turkey is done, transfer to a platter, cover with aluminum foil, and allow to rest 15 minutes. To serve, slice diagonally on the bias.

1 (6-pound) bone-in turkey breast

1 recipe Poultry Brine (recipe follows)

¾ cup Jay D's Spicy & Sweet Barbecue Rub (purchased or recipe page 183, or your favorite commercial brand), divided

1 cup (2 sticks) unsalted butter

2 quarts cold water

½ cup kosher salt

½ cup sugar

2 tablespoons paprika

2 tablespoons chili powder

2 tablespoons garlic powder

1 tablespoon onion powder

1 teaspoon cayenne pepper

1 teaspoon ground white pepper

# POULTRY BRINE

MAKES 2 QUARTS

Place all ingredients in a large saucepan and bring to a simmer. When salt and sugar are dissolved, turn off the heat. Cool brine completely before using.

Turkey chili.

# TURKEY CHILI WITH SWEET POTATOES AND BLACK BEANS

MAKES 4–6 SERVINGS

**This is a good recipe for using up leftover Thanksgiving turkey.**

**1.** Heat a large saucepan over the medium heat of a propane burner or your stove and add olive oil, onion, garlic, bell pepper, and jalapeños. Sauté until onion just turns translucent, 3–5 minutes.

**2.** Add sweet potatoes, chicken stock, tomatoes, chili powder, barbecue rub, cumin, and oregano. Simmer until sweet potatoes are almost tender, about 20 minutes.

**3.** Stir in shredded turkey and black beans. Simmer another 15 minutes. Season with salt and pepper to taste and serve hot in bowls.

1 tablespoon olive oil

1 large onion, diced

5 cloves garlic, minced

1 large bell pepper, seeded and diced

2 jalapeño peppers, seeded and diced

1½ pounds sweet potatoes, peeled and diced

1 quart chicken stock

1 (28-ounce) can diced tomatoes, with liquid

2 tablespoons chili powder

2 tablespoons Jay D's Spicy & Sweet Barbecue Rub (purchased or recipe page 183, or your favorite commercial brand)

1 tablespoon cumin

1 teaspoon dried oregano

1½ pounds (5–6 cups) shredded cooked turkey

1 (15-ounce) can black beans, drained and rinsed

Salt and ground black pepper

# GLAZED JALAPEÑO DUCK POPPERS

MAKES 10-12 HORS D'OEUVRES

3 slices bacon, cut into thirds crosswise

½ cup Jay D's Louisiana Barbecue Sauce (purchased or recipe page 186, or your favorite commercial brand), divided

¼ cup cream cheese

1 wild or domestic duck breast, sliced into ¼-inch slices (should be 10–12 slices)

10 fresh jalapeño pepper slices, seeded and veins removed

Toothpicks

**1.** Prepare an outdoor grill to medium-high direct and indirect heat, or heat your oven to 400°F. Lay bacon in a cast-iron skillet or on a sheet pan and grill, fry, or bake until just starting to turn brown, 7–8 minutes. Set aside and let cool. Combine 3 tablespoons barbecue sauce with cream cheese. Set aside.

**2.** Slightly flatten duck breast slices, and center one slice on top of each piece of bacon. Spoon a teaspoonful of the cream cheese mixture onto each piece of duck. Top each with a jalapeño slice. Roll the bacon up and over the poppers and secure with toothpicks.

**3.** For grilling, place poppers in a large cast-iron skillet and partially cook for 7 minutes over indirect heat. Transfer poppers directly to the grates over the hottest part of the grill. Cook and baste with the remaining barbecue sauce until the duck is medium rare and the bacon is just done and crispy. Should take about 5 more minutes. If cooking in the oven, baste every 5 minutes until done, about 15 minutes. Serve warm.

# WILD DUCK AND OYSTER GUMBO

MAKES 8-10 SERVINGS

**The secret to cooking oysters is to not cook them too long, or they'll get rubbery.**

**1.** Liberally season the ducks with salt and pepper. Set a propane burner or your stove to medium heat, and cook ducks in a large cast-iron skillet until most of the fat has rendered out and the skin is nice and crispy. Reserve the rendered fat. When cool enough to handle, pick the meat and skin from the ducks and roughly chop into 1$\frac{1}{2}$-inch pieces. Discard bone and skin and set the meat aside.

**2.** To make the roux, heat 1 cup of reserved duck fat in a cast-iron Dutch oven over a medium flame. Add the flour and cook slowly, stirring constantly, until mixture is a light golden brown, about 30 minutes. If roux cooks too fast, lower the heat. Continue cooking until roux turns the color of milk chocolate, about 5 more minutes.

**3.** Stir in onions and cook, stirring constantly, until the roux takes on a deep dark chocolate color, another 5–10 minutes. Stir in the duck, andouille, celery, and garlic and cook 5 minutes, stirring frequently.

**4.** Add broth, oyster liquor, okra, Creole seasoning, Worcestershire sauce, and bay leaves, and bring to a boil. Reduce heat and simmer, uncovered, until flavors marry, about 1$\frac{1}{2}$ hours. Occasionally skim the fat that rises to the top.

**5.** Add the oysters and simmer 5 minutes. Add Tabasco sauce and season to taste with salt and pepper. Serve in soup bowls hot over rice garnished with sliced green onion.

2 wild ducks (2$\frac{1}{2}$-3 pounds each), skin on, quartered

Salt and pepper to taste

1 cup duck fat (store-bought), or lard or vegetable oil

1 cup all-purpose flour

2 large onions, diced

1 pound andouille sausage, cut into $\frac{1}{2}$-inch slices

3 stalks celery, chopped

2 tablespoons minced garlic

12 cups duck or chicken broth

2 cups oyster liquor from 2 pints fresh oysters (reserve oysters)

2 cups sliced fresh or frozen okra

3 tablespoons Creole seasoning (purchased or recipe page 182)

1 tablespoon Worcestershire sauce

2 bay leaves

1$\frac{1}{2}$ teaspoons Tabasco sauce

For serving: hot cooked rice (recipe page 166), and $\frac{1}{2}$ cup chopped green onion

# BOUDIN STUFFED QUAIL WITH CRANBERRY BOURBON SAUCE

Canola oil

1/2 pound ground pork

1/4 pound chicken livers, finely chopped

1/2 cup diced yellow onion

1/4 cup diced green bell pepper

1/4 cup diced celery

2 cloves garlic, minced

Cajun seasoning (purchased or recipe page 182)

2 cups cooked rice (recipe page 166)

2 green onions, diced

4 semi-boneless quail

For serving: Cranberry Bourbon Sauce (recipe follows)

**Consider this recipe for your next holiday gathering. The stuffing is a simple homemade boudin that's also spectacular stuffed in turkey, chicken, and duck.**

**1.** Lightly coat a medium sauté pan with canola oil. Over the medium-high heat of a propane burner or your stove, brown the ground pork and chicken livers 5 minutes. Add the onion, bell pepper, and celery and sauté until vegetables are sweated, another 5 minutes. Add the garlic and continue to sauté a few more minutes. Season with Cajun seasoning to taste.

**2.** Remove mixture from the heat, and fold in the cooked rice and green onion until everything is well incorporated. You now have boudin. Reserve to the side.

**3.** Preheat a grill for medium-high direct and indirect heat, or heat up your oven to 350°F. Season the outside and inside of each quail with Cajun seasoning. On oiled grill grates set over direct heat, sear the quail on each side, about 3–5 minutes per side. On your stove, sear over medium-high heat in a few tablespoons oil in a skillet. Remove the quail from the heat and allow to cool enough to handle.

**4.** Stuff each quail with as much boudin as can fit inside the cavities. Breast side up, place stuffed quail over indirect grill heat or in a pan in the oven. Roast with the grill covered until fully cooked, about 10–15 minutes. Serve the quail hot with the Cranberry Bourbon Sauce.

# CRANBERRY BOURBON SAUCE

MAKES ABOUT 1½ CUPS

**This outrageously simple sauce makes plain cuts of pork, chicken, or game taste restaurant quality.**

**1.** In a small sauce pot set over medium heat, add the cranberries and sugar and enough water to cover the berries. Bring to a boil and simmer until cranberries begin to break down, about 10–15 minutes. Remove from heat.

**2.** When cool enough, transfer mixture to a blender. Add the bourbon and puree until smooth. Serve warm or at room temperature. Can be kept in the refrigerator up to a week.

1 cup fresh cranberries

½ cup sugar

Water

½ cup bourbon

# SMOTHERED DOVES

MAKES 4 SERVINGS

8 wild doves (2–3 pounds),
cleaned and cut in half

1 cup all-purpose flour

Canola oil for pan frying

1 cup chopped onion

1 cup chopped celery

3 tablespoons minced garlic

6 cups cold chicken broth

For serving: hot cooked rice
(recipe page 166)

Seasoning blend:

2 teaspoons salt

1 teaspoon onion powder

1 teaspoon smoked paprika

1 teaspoon garlic powder

3/4 teaspoon white pepper

1/2 teaspoon cayenne

1/2 teaspoon black pepper

1/2 teaspoon dried basil

1/2 teaspoon filé powder (optional)

**This is one of the few dishes other than gumbo that I think tastes good with filé.**

**1.** Mix together seasoning-blend ingredients in a small bowl. Sprinkle 2 teaspoons on dove pieces and massage into the skin.

**2.** In a large shallow bowl, combine 2 1/2 teaspoons of seasoning blend with the flour. Dredge dove pieces in seasoned flour and set aside. Reserve leftover flour.

**3.** Over the medium-high heat of a propane burner or your stove, heat 1/4 inch oil in a cast-iron Dutch oven to 350°F. Add doves and cook until golden brown on both sides. Remove doves and set aside. Pour off all but 1/2 cup of the hot oil from pot. Make a roux by whisking in reserved seasoned flour and cooking and stirring constantly until the roux turns dark brown.

**4.** Stir in onion, celery, and garlic. Add broth and bring to a boil. Add doves, lower heat to a simmer, cover the pot, and cook until tender, 1–1 1/2 hours. Liquid should have reduced to about 4 cups. Serve doves on plates alongside hot rice covered with dove gravy.

# WILD GAME

I learned to shoot like most six-year-olds, first with a BB gun, later with a pellet gun, and after that with .22 rifles and pistols. And, as with most kids around here, my first game target was squirrels. Even in Louisiana's large cities, there's a deranged number of squirrels. The two most common are the gray squirrel, also known as the cat squirrel, and the fox squirrel, or red squirrel. Out in the woods, it's pretty easy to find the gnawed pine cone, acorn, and pecan shells squirrels drop. Just look up in the trees nearby, and the messy squirrels will be leering down at you.

When I was a boy, after many a crisp fall day in the woods, I would bring my skinned squirrels back to my Granny, who would smother them in gravy and serve them over rice. This was a dish that always made this young hunter proud.

I began hunting larger game during my elementary and high school years, when my family lived in Texas. Our various hunting trips typically ended up with limits of whitetail deer, feral hogs, and cottontail rabbits. The most unusual thing I've ever bagged was a rattlesnake. I was only about thirteen years old when my brother, two of our south Texas friends, and I shot a seven-foot diamondback. Without thinking twice, we skinned and gutted the reptile, cut it into small sections, seasoned it, and grilled it over mesquite. Since that day, I've eaten rattlesnake many times. I have some in my freezer right now. Snake is actually quite tasty. I'm so fond of it that once, at a Baton Rouge pop-up dinner, I served some python I found online. The meat on a snake sits on top of the rib cage on each side, and it is pink when raw and white when cooked. To me, snake tastes like a cross between alligator and a free-range chicken, only a little stringier.

Another cold-blooded critter that crawls all over Louisiana's marshes is the alligator. Our state has the nation's highest population of this ancient creature, with close to two million out in the wild. Several decades ago, unregulated harvesting almost wiped them out, and in 1962, the season was closed. Thankfully, the state of Louisiana implemented a sustained use program that

Jay and friends holding
a rattlesnake.

regulates harvest, bolsters the survival of the species, maintains habitat, and gives an economic benefit and incentive to the folks in the alligator business. Beginning in the early 1970s, the season was gradually reinstated. Today, we harvest over 300,000 wild and farmed alligators annually. Conservationists recognize this success story worldwide. I've never been on an alligator hunt, but if the opportunity comes up, I won't turn it down. Frozen alligator tail meat is sold here in seafood markets, and I like to cut it into nuggets and blacken or fry it. When I really want something different, I pull out by big cast-iron cauldron and simmer alligator in white beans, which I first did with my cousin Travis at a Third Row Tailgate party.

## Outlaw Pigs and Rodents

It's been many years since I hunted feral swine (sometimes called boars) in Texas, and maybe it's time I seriously think about doing the same in Louisiana. Like so many other states, ours has a serious wild hog problem. Officially classified as outlaw quadrupeds, these dark, hairy, tusked pigs have no natural predators. They seek places with easy access to water and food, and over a half-million roam the state's tidal marshes, hardwood forests, and pastures. Recently in New Orleans, over a dozen were even found rooting around busy City Park.

As in much of the South, hogs have been running wild in Louisiana since colonial times, when many of the domestic pigs the Spanish brought to North America escaped and became feral. Around the year 1900, a new non-domestic batch was brought over for sport from Europe, and many of them evaded hunters and reproduced. A large part of the wild pig population trampling around south Louisiana today, however, came here from Texas in the 1970s, again, as wild boars destined for hunting. Some of that group escaped from pens in Chalmette, right below New Orleans, and have since been briskly breeding and creating havoc.

Whatever their pedigree, wild boars are destructive. They root through the levees that protect us from hurricanes, and they have been known to attack sheep and cattle. They also ruin commercial crops, such as sugarcane, rice, and soybeans, and in 2013 were the cause of an estimated $74 million in damage to farms.

The good news is that wild boar is tasty. The Louisiana Department of Wildlife and Fisheries allows holders of a valid Louisiana hunting license to hunt feral hogs year-round during legal daylight shooting hours. With the appropriate permits and notifications, the law also provides for hunting wild hogs at night. I must say, grilled wild hog loin is delectable. The ground-up tougher cuts make outstanding sausage.

An equally destructive animal is the nutria. This aquatic rodent has a hairless tail and an exaggerated bright orange overbite, and adults easily grow to twenty pounds. Nutria have ravenous appetites and gnaw on the roots and stems of the marsh plants in Louisiana's coastal wetlands, forming permanent flooded ponds and destroying wildlife habitat.

Like feral hogs, the nutria is not native to the state. This invasive species was brought here for their fur from Argentina in the 1930s. A few escaped and quickly bred themselves into a population of millions that has turned much of our wetlands into high-salinity wastelands.

There have been several government efforts to curb the nutria population. The latest try encourages hunters and trappers to bag them and bring the severed tails in for a six-dollar bounty. This program has been encouraging. For years, officials have also been begging diners to give nutria a try. Nutria meat is lean, low in cholesterol, and tastes like a cross between pork and turkey. Unfortunately, the idea of nutria for dinner hasn't caught on. Maybe it's because they're so new to our ecosystem that folks here think of them as foreign. Or maybe the turnoff is the thought of those orange buckteeth.

## Mad for Whitetails

I grew up spending every Thanksgiving morning clutching my father's .30-06 in a deer stand. The species common in Louisiana and Texas is the white-tailed deer. I shot my first whitetail buck in south Texas when I was eleven or twelve years old. I had that ten-point's head mounted, and my family and I ate the rest. For the next six years I did lots of deer hunting with my father and brother in the Texas deserts. The usual routine was to stalk deer during the day. At night, we'd camp out in the open. I usually volunteered to start a mesquite fire in a hole in the dirt or in a firepit made from an old tractor-tire rim, and I'd cook whatever was on the evening menu.

**Jay on *MasterChef*.**

Unfortunately, hunting season for both birds and wild game overlaps with football season, so these days I don't hunt for my favorite target, deer, as much as I used to. But I still manage to get out in the woods a few times a year, which keeps my freezer well stocked. If I accidentally run low on the supply from my hunts, I raid my dad's freezer. I try to always have venison on hand.

## Venison on National TV

In 2011, during my first national television appearance on Fox's *MasterChef*, I chose to prepare an herb-roasted rack of venison with a Cajun shrimp and cornbread-stuffed bell pepper. For me, cooking venison in this contest was a natural, since the meat is something considered different, yet I grew up eating it. Most importantly, I'd cooked it hundreds of times.

Even though I bought this particular rack from Whole Foods, on the show I cooked it the way I'd prepare a buck I shot myself. The main difference was that I topped this piece with a bourbon cream sauce. And, yes, I took a couple of shots of bourbon while I was cooking. (Hey, it was a fellow contestant's birthday!) After the first shot, a producer came running from across the warehouse set, screaming and seemingly upset. "Did you just take a shot of that?" she asked. I couldn't say no. "Yes, it's his birthday," I explained defensively. "Well, we didn't get it on camera. Can you do it again?" she pleaded. Twist my arm.

I was confident in my cooking, yet I was concerned about wowing the judges, Gordon Ramsay, Joe Bastianich, and Graham Elliot, who, to me, were culinary rock stars. I'll never forget the conversation I had with Gordon Ramsay, which happened right before I plated, when I was getting ready to slice my perfectly cooked venison. He sat back in his chair and said, "You look like a chef. You talk like a chef. Let's hope you cook like a chef." I was floored. Gordon Ramsay was complimenting me. "Let's hope I do," I said.

Ramsay judged me first. He cut into the stuffing in the middle of my bell pepper and took a taste. He promptly handed me a clean fork to taste my own food, and my heart sank. I took a nibble and realized it was terribly bland. I said, "It needs more salt, Chef." He exclaimed, "It needs more everything!" He then tasted the venison and a dribble of the bourbon cream sauce. He seemed to like the venison, but as he walked away, he said something along the lines of, "The venison's cooked perfectly but the bell pepper is bland. . . . What a shame, what a shame." Elliot and Bastianich shared Ramsay's bleak opinion.

I'll admit it, I made a few mistakes—I didn't adjust for the taste and texture of the store-bought California cornbread, my bell pepper seasoning was off, and my plating could have been much more attractive. So I didn't advance and try for the title of MasterChef, but at least the judges liked the venison.

That failure was painful, and at this point, I could have easily quit chasing my culinary dream. Instead I took it as a lesson, and I ran with it. I knew that, if I wanted to make a living in the food world, I still had a lot to learn. So I used the loss to fuel the next four years of my life, which involved a lot of practicing, and I eventually made it all the way up to *Food Network Star.*

## Camp, Sweet Camp

Like many Louisiana families, mine proudly cooks any animal we take while hunting. When I was growing up, we'd usually do the cooking right away at our hunting camp. Many, many years ago, my Grandpa Ducote, who was a carpenter, built our camp upriver from Simmesport, in Avoyelles Parish, on the eastern side of Central Louisiana. To reach our piece of wooded paradise, we'd put a flat-bottomed aluminum boat in at the Atchafalaya River and motor north about five miles into the Red River, where the camp still sits on its muddy banks.

The Ducote Family Camp is a glorified two-story cabin made mostly of cypress. It has a dirt floor and a wood-burning stove, and rain furnishes its water for toilets. The camp also doesn't have electricity; for light, we use Coleman lanterns and the glow of a fire. Some of my happiest memories were made in that rustic cabin. Using our cast-iron stove, my father taught me how to cook squirrel stew, rice and gravy, and biscuits in the morning. This was the place where I learned how to properly grill steaks. It's also the place where the surrounding darkness, the woodsy scent of the trees, the croaking of frogs, and a brisk winter cold snap just seem to make everything taste better.

# TURTLE SOUP

MAKES 8 SERVINGS

1 gallon water

2 pounds turtle meat

4 bay leaves

2 tablespoons beef base paste
(Better Than Bouillon is a good
brand)

1½ teaspoons whole cloves

1½ teaspoons whole black
peppercorns

1½ teaspoons dried thyme

1 tablespoon butter

3 cups diced onion

2 cups diced bell pepper

2 cups diced celery

1 quart tomato juice

1 (10-ounce) can diced tomatoes
and green chilis

½ cup Worcestershire sauce

¼ cup Tabasco sauce

2 tablespoons minced fresh garlic

1 tablespoon granulated onion

1 tablespoon coarse ground black
pepper

1 cup vegetable oil

1 cup all-purpose flour

1 cup sherry

**Adapted from a recipe by Chef Eusebio Gongora, a good friend and the co-owner of Southern Poké restaurants in Baton Rouge and Lafayette.**

**1.** Put the water in a large stock pot and add the turtle, bay leaves, beef base, cloves, peppercorns, and thyme. Simmer over a propane burner or your stove until turtle is tender, about 1½ hours. Strain meat and reserve stock. Once meat has cooled, run through a grinder or rough chop by hand.

**2.** In a large Dutch oven set over medium-high heat, melt butter and sauté onion, bell pepper, and celery until soft, about 6 minutes. Add tomato juice and canned diced tomatoes and green chilis and cook 10 minutes. Add reserved stock, ground meat, Worcestershire sauce, Tabasco sauce, garlic, granulated onion, and black pepper, and simmer 45 minutes.

**3.** Make a blonde roux by first putting a heavy-bottomed skillet over a medium flame. Mix the oil and flour in the skillet and stir constantly until roux just begins to take on color, about 5–7 minutes.

**4.** Add the roux to the soup and simmer, uncovered, until slightly thick, about 30 minutes. Stir in the sherry and cook an additional 10 minutes. Serve hot in shallow soup bowls.

# WILD BOAR GRILLADES AND GRAVY

MAKES 8–10 SERVINGS

Grillades are pieces of meat that are seared and simmered in a rich gravy. In New Orleans, beef, veal, and pork grillades are usually pounded into thin medallions before they're seared. In southwest Louisiana, grillades are typically cut into chunks and left that way.

**1.** Heat the olive oil in a large heavy saucepan. Add the bell pepper, white and green onions, celery, and garlic. Sauté until things begin to brown, about 8 minutes.

**2.** Add the tomatoes, bay leaves, salt, and pepper and mix thoroughly. Add the stock and Worcestershire sauce and cook, stirring and skimming frequently, for 5 minutes. Stir in the cornstarch slurry and adjust the seasoning with salt and pepper. Set aside.

**3.** Cook rice and keep warm.

**4.** After rice is cooked and sitting covered, mix together the flour and Creole seasoning in a shallow bowl. Dredge the boar cubes in the seasoned flour. Heat canola oil in a heavy skillet and sear the meat on each side until browned. Put the meat into the sauce and simmer until it's fully cooked, about 20 minutes.

**5.** To serve, mound rice in individual serving bowls and top with meat and sauce. Garnish with chopped parsley.

¾ cup olive oil

3 cups finely chopped green bell pepper

3 cups finely chopped white onion

2 cups thinly sliced green onion

3 ribs celery, finely chopped

5 cloves garlic, minced

8 small ripe tomatoes, seeded and finely chopped

3 bay leaves

2½ teaspoons kosher salt

½ teaspoon freshly ground black pepper

2 quarts beef stock

2 tablespoons Worcestershire sauce

4 tablespoons cornstarch mixed with ½ cup cold water

3 cups uncooked long-grain rice (recipe page 166)

2 cups all-purpose flour

2 teaspoons Creole seasoning (purchased or recipe page 182)

5 pounds wild boar shoulder, cut into 2-inch cubes

3 tablespoons canola oil

For serving: 1 bunch fresh parsley, chopped

# GRILLED RATTLESNAKE

MAKES 4 SERVINGS (BEGIN A DAY AHEAD)

1 (4-foot) rattlesnake

2 heaping tablespoons Jay D's Spicy & Sweet Barbecue Rub (purchased or recipe page 183, or your favorite commercial brand)

2 (12- to 17-inch) metal skewers

**Did you know that rattlesnake is the most consumed culinary snake in the United States? Old-time cowboys frequently used rattlers to make chili. I like mine grilled. Rattlesnake meat is easy to find on the Internet. If you hunt your own, be sure to stay away from the fangs, even if the snake no longer moves. (For this recipe, the seasoning and cooking times vary greatly depending on the size of the snake.)**

**1.** Skin and gut the snake. Soak the snake in water overnight in the refrigerator.

**2.** When ready to cook, remove snake from the water and pat dry. Heat a covered grill to medium-high. Rub the snake with the barbecue rub, then coil it on itself. Skewer the snake so that it stays together in a spiral.

**3.** Place the coiled snake, rib side down, on the hot grill. Close the grill's lid. For a 4-foot snake, cook 5 minutes. Flip and grill another 5 minutes. (Remember, smaller snakes take less cooking time. A good test for doneness is when the meat easily pulls off the bone.)

**4.** Remove from heat and let rest 5 minutes. The meat will peel off the backbone and ribs in large patches. Pick it clean with your fingers and enjoy.

# RUSTIC SQUIRREL STEW

MAKES 8 SERVINGS

**This is the basic way my grandmother cooked squirrel, in a dark, thick gravy that's ladled over rice.**

1. Place a small heavy skillet over the medium heat of a propane burner or stove. Make a dark roux by adding 3 tablespoons oil and the flour and stirring constantly until dark brown, about 12 minutes. Remove roux to another pot or a heat-safe bowl to stop cooking.

2. Place a large cast-iron pot with a heavy lid over medium-high heat and add the 1/4 cup oil. While the oil is heating, sprinkle the squirrel pieces with all of the Cajun seasoning. Cooking in batches, lay the squirrel in the hot oil and brown well on all sides. Remove browned pieces to a plate.

3. Add the sausage, onion, celery, and bell pepper to the pot and sauté until the onion begins to brown, about 8 minutes. Add the garlic and deglaze the pot with the wine and Worcestershire. Cook until some of the alcohol burns off, about 5 minutes. Stir in the chicken stock, mushrooms, the prepared roux, salt, pepper, and hot sauce. Lower heat to a simmer, cover the pot, and cook 1 hour.

4. Uncover and check the level of the liquid. It should barely cover the squirrel. Add water if needed. Cover and cook until the squirrel is fork tender and the gravy thickens to coat the back of a spoon, about another hour. (This would be a good time to cook the rice.)

5. Taste the gravy and adjust for seasoning. Serve over a mound of hot rice garnished with green onion.

1/4 cup vegetable oil, plus 3 tablespoons

3 tablespoons all-purpose flour

4 squirrels, cleaned and cut into serving-sized pieces

2 1/2 tablespoons Cajun seasoning (purchased or recipe page 182)

2 cups chopped smoked pork sausage, in bite-sized pieces

2 cups diced yellow onion

1 cup diced celery

1 cup diced bell pepper

3 tablespoons minced garlic

1 cup dry red wine

1 1/2 tablespoons Worcestershire sauce

1 quart chicken stock

2 cups button mushrooms, halved

Kosher salt and black pepper to taste

Hot sauce to taste

For serving: hot cooked rice (recipe page 166) and 1 1/4 cups diced green onion tops

Blackened alligator.

# BLACKENED ALLIGATOR NUGGETS

MAKES 8 SERVINGS

**1.** Place a large cast-iron skillet over the high heat of a propane burner or stove and allow it to get screaming hot. Toss the alligator meat in enough seasoning to coat each piece. Reserve the remaining seasoning for another use.

**2.** Add the canola oil to the skillet and drop the alligator in. Do not move or stir. Allow the alligator to stick to the skillet and it will release itself when it's done, within minutes. Flip each piece over and blacken it on the other side until it releases, approximately 1–2 minutes.

**3.** Remove alligator from the skillet and serve hot with a dipping sauce of your choice, such as white remoulade or Jay D's Louisiana Molasses Mustard.

2 pounds alligator tail meat, diced into ¼-inch chunks

Blackening Seasoning (recipe follows)

1 tablespoon canola oil

Jay D's Louisiana Molasses Mustard (purchased or recipe page 184)

# BLACKENING SEASONING

MAKES APPROXIMATELY 1 CUP

Combine all ingredients in a bowl. Store in a covered container up to 12 months.

3 tablespoons smoked paprika

2 tablespoons ancho chili powder

2 tablespoons dried granulated onion

2 tablespoons dried granulated garlic

2 tablespoons finely ground black pepper

1 tablespoon cayenne pepper

1 tablespoon white pepper

1 tablespoon kosher salt

2 teaspoons ground thyme

2 teaspoons ground oregano

# GRILLED RABBIT

MAKES 4 SERVINGS

1 (3- to 4-pound) wild or domestic rabbit, dressed

½ cup olive oil, plus more for brushing grill

3 large cloves garlic, coarsely chopped

Zest and juice from 1 lemon

2 teaspoons fresh oregano leaves

1 teaspoon fresh rosemary leaves, plus a few sprigs for garnish

1 teaspoon light molasses or honey

½ teaspoon salt

½ teaspoon ground black pepper

¼ teaspoon cayenne pepper

From Louisiana woodland hares to Texas brush cottontails, I've spent many an hour stalking rabbits with a .22 long rifle. Sprinting rabbits are good target practice, but they also make a good meal. Even if they weren't so tasty, I'd find a way to make them edible; it's always been my golden rule that whatever I bag goes into the pot.

**1.** Cut rabbit into 8 serving pieces. Place in a large bowl or resealable food-safe plastic bag. Make a marinade by placing remaining ingredients in the bowl of a food processor or in a blender and process until fairly smooth. Coat rabbit with marinade, cover the bowl, and refrigerate 2 hours.

**2.** Heat a grill to medium-high heat. Brush the hot grate with olive oil. Remove rabbit from marinade and shake off excess. Reserve marinade. First grill large pieces, such as legs, for 10 minutes, turning occasionally. Toss on the smaller pieces, such as the loin and ribs, and grill everything 20 minutes. Turn every 5 minutes and baste with reserved marinade. Transfer cooked rabbit to a warm platter, garnish with rosemary sprigs, and serve warm.

# BUTTERMILK FRIED RABBIT

MAKES 4 SERVINGS

**1.** In a very large bowl, mix together the buttermilk, hot sauce, green onion, garlic powder, and oregano. Plop in the rabbit pieces, and use a large spoon or your hands to coat them well. Cover and refrigerate at least 8 hours or overnight.

**2.** When ready to cook, pour 4 inches oil into a Dutch oven. Heat oil over the medium heat of a propane burner or stove until it reaches 350°F. Meanwhile, in a large paper bag or food-safe plastic bag, combine the flour, paprika, chili powder, salt, black pepper, and cayenne. Add half of rabbit and shake in the bag until well-coated.

**3.** Shake off excess flour mixture, and drop rabbit pieces into hot oil. Fry 8 minutes on one side and turn. Fry another 5 minutes. Meat should be golden brown. If you're not sure it's done, test with a thermometer to be sure it's up to 165°F. (Larger pieces will take a minute or two longer.)

**4.** Drain rabbit on paper towels. Mound onto a platter, decorate with parsley sprigs, and serve warm.

2 cups well-shaken buttermilk

2 tablespoons Louisiana-style hot sauce

1 tablespoon minced green onion

1 teaspoon garlic powder

½ teaspoon dried oregano

2 wild or domestic rabbits, dressed, each cut into 6 pieces

Vegetable oil for frying

1½ cups all-purpose flour

1 tablespoon paprika

1 tablespoon chili powder

2 teaspoons kosher salt

2 teaspoons ground black pepper

1 teaspoon cayenne pepper

For serving: parsley sprigs

# RABBIT STEW WITH POTATOES AND CARROTS

MAKES 8 SERVINGS

2 wild or domestic dressed rabbits (3 pounds total), cut into serving pieces

1 cup all-purpose flour, plus 5 tablespoons

6 tablespoons butter

3 medium onions, thinly sliced

2 cups diced celery

1 tablespoon minced garlic

2½ quarts water or chicken stock

1 tablespoon fresh thyme leaves

2 teaspoons kosher salt

1 teaspoon ground black pepper

2 bay leaves

4 cups coarsely chopped carrots

9 small red potatoes, quartered

8 ounces mushrooms, sliced

2 tablespoons cornstarch mixed with 2 tablespoons water

For serving: hot cooked rice (recipe page 166)

**1.** Dust rabbit pieces with 1 cup of flour. Melt butter in a cast-iron Dutch oven set over the medium flame of a propane burner or stove. Brown flour-dusted rabbit on all sides. Remove from pot and set aside.

**2.** To the same pot, add onions, celery, and garlic. Sauté until tender, about 7 minutes. Stir in remaining 5 tablespoons flour and stir constantly to make a blonde roux, about 7 to 8 minutes.

**3.** Whisk in water, thyme, salt, pepper, and bay leaves. Put rabbit back into Dutch oven and bring to a boil. Reduce to a simmer and cook, covered, 2 hours.

**4.** Add carrots, potatoes, and mushrooms, and cook uncovered until vegetables are tender, another 30–35 minutes. To thicken, whisk in the cornstarch slurry and simmer 2 minutes. Serve stew hot over cooked rice.

# VENISON GRILLADES

**1.** Remove and discard any fat or sinew tissue on the venison. Cut the steak into 2-inch squares. Combine the salt, cayenne, and black pepper in a small bowl.

**2.** On a sturdy cutting board, pound each piece of meat with a meat mallet until slightly flattened. Sprinkle all pieces with some of the seasoning mix and a little flour. Turn the pieces over and apply seasoning and flour, then pound that side too. Repeat until all the meat has been seasoned and flattened.

**3.** In a large, heavy pot set over a propane burner or your stove, heat the oil over medium heat. Working in batches, brown the venison pieces on both sides. After all the meat is browned, remove it to a plate.

**4.** To the same pot, add the onion, bell pepper, celery, and garlic. Stir over medium heat until the vegetables are soft, about 10 minutes. Return the meat to the pot. Add the tomatoes, beef broth, bay leaves, and half the parsley. Stir everything together, and cover the pot. Bring to a boil; then reduce to a simmer and cook, partially covered and stirring occasionally, until the meat is tender, about an hour.

**5.** Remove the bay leaves. Add the remaining half of the parsley and cook 5 more minutes. Garnish with green onion. Serve hot over grits or rice.

4 pounds boneless venison round steak

1 tablespoon kosher salt

1 teaspoon cayenne pepper

1 teaspoon ground black pepper

½ cup all-purpose flour

½ cup vegetable oil

1 large yellow onion, finely diced

1 green bell pepper, finely diced

2 stalks celery, finely diced

5 cloves garlic, minced

2 Creole tomatoes, diced

3 cups beef broth

3 bay leaves

½ cup chopped parsley, divided

For serving: hot cooked rice (recipe page 166) or hot grits, and ½ cup finely chopped green onion

# GRILLED VENISON BACKSTRAP WITH GREEN CHIMICHURRI SAUCE

MAKES 4-6 SERVINGS

1 (2- to 3-pound) venison backstrap or beef tenderloin

1 tablespoon olive oil

1 tablespoon kosher salt

Freshly ground black pepper to taste

For serving: Green Chimichurri Sauce (recipe follows)

**1.** Take meat out of the refrigerator 30 minutes before cooking. Heat a covered grill to high heat. Remove the silverskin (the silvery colored connective tissue) from the backstrap. Pat the meat dry with paper towels. Rub on the olive oil, salt, and pepper. Grill over direct heat, with lid closed, for 4 minutes. Turn the meat and grill, with cover closed, for 3 minutes.

**2.** Reduce heat to low and grill with lid closed for 4–7 minutes (4 minutes for rare and 7 minutes for medium). Remove from heat and let stand 10 minutes before slicing.

**3.** To serve, cut meat into thin slices and serve with Green Chimichurri Sauce.

# GREEN CHIMICHURRI SAUCE

MAKES ABOUT 1 CUP

**This sauce adds exciting flavor to any grilled meat.**

**1.** Mix together the olive oil and lemon juice and set aside. In the bowl of a food processor, add the parsley, onion, garlic, oregano, salt, black pepper, and red pepper. Pulse until finely chopped.

**2.** Keep the motor running and drizzle in the olive oil mixture. When everything is combined well, transfer the chimichurri to a bowl, cover, and refrigerate at least 3 hours. Can be made a day ahead.

½ cup extra virgin olive oil

¼ cup freshly squeezed lemon juice

1 cup packed parsley leaves

¼ cup finely chopped white onion

2 tablespoons minced garlic

2 tablespoons fresh oregano

1 teaspoon kosher salt

¼ teaspoon freshly ground black pepper

¼ teaspoon crushed red pepper

Venison and chimi.

# CHICKEN FRIED VENISON BACKSTRAP WITH CORN GRAVY

MAKES 8 SERVINGS (BEGIN A DAY AHEAD)

1 (2-pound) venison backstrap

1 quart buttermilk

1 tablespoon olive oil

1 shallot, minced

3 garlic cloves, minced

2 cups corn kernels, cut fresh from the cob

1 red bell pepper, small-diced

3 sprigs thyme

2 cups heavy cream

2 tablespoons cornstarch, plus 2 tablespoons cold water to make a slurry

2 cups all-purpose flour

2 cups panko breadcrumbs

2 tablespoons Creole seasoning (purchased or recipe page 182, or your favorite commercial brand)

⅓ cup canola oil

**1.** Cut venison into ½-inch slices, and soak in buttermilk overnight in the refrigerator.

**2.** When ready to cook, first make corn gravy. Place a heavy saucepan over the medium heat of a propane burner or your stove and add the olive oil. Add shallot and sauté until soft, 3–4 minutes. Add garlic and sauté just until fragrant, about 30 seconds. Add corn kernels, bell pepper, and thyme and cook until corn is soft, about 10 minutes. Add cream and cornstarch slurry and stir frequently until gravy reaches simmer. Cook 2 minutes. Cover, remove the gravy from the heat, and keep it warm.

**3.** Remove venison from buttermilk and place the buttermilk used for soaking in a large shallow bowl. In another shallow bowl, combine the flour, breadcrumbs, and Creole seasoning. In a heavy-bottomed skillet, heat canola oil to 350°F.

**4.** While oil is heating, pound each venison steak to ¼ inch. Dip each piece in the buttermilk, then in the breading mixture. Fry until golden brown, about 2–3 minutes per side. To serve, place a slice of warm venison on a dinner plate, and top with corn gravy.

# ELK SAUSAGE AND BLACK BEAN SOUP

MAKES 8 SERVINGS

Although historians think elk may have roamed parts of north Louisiana centuries ago, as far as I know, they don't exist anywhere around here now. But way back when I lived with my parents, our freezer was always stocked with plenty of elk cutlets, elk sausage, and ground elk, all from my dad's hunting trips to Colorado and New Mexico. Today, I always have cuts from large, antlered Rocky Mountain elk in my own freezer, and they are a staple for my grill and chili pots.

**1.** In a Dutch oven set over the medium-high heat of a propane burner or stove, add 3 tablespoons olive oil, and brown elk sausage well on all sides Remove the sausage and set aside to cool. Add the remaining 3 tablespoons olive oil and butter to the same pot. Stir until butter melts. Add the flour and stir with a wooden spoon constantly to make a dark brown roux, about 10 minutes.

**2.** To the roux in the pot, add the onion and stir 1 minute. Add the bell pepper and celery and stir another minute. Stir in the garlic and serrano pepper. Carefully add the black beans, with their liquid, and the chicken broth.

**3.** Cut the elk sausage into 1/4-inch slices and add to the pot. Add the Cajun seasoning, salt, black pepper, bay leaves, thyme, cumin, and paprika. Bring the soup to a boil, reduce to a simmer, and cook 1/2 hour, stirring occasionally. Add the green onion and simmer another 1/2 hour, stirring occasionally.

**4.** Taste and adjust seasonings. When ready to serve, remove the bay leaves, ladle hot soup into bowls, and garnish with parsley and cilantro.

6 tablespoons olive oil, divided

1 pound link elk sausage

2 tablespoons unsalted butter

1/2 cup all-purpose flour

1 medium yellow onion, diced

1 green bell pepper, diced

2 stalks celery, diced

4 cloves garlic, minced

3 serrano peppers, seeded and minced

3 (19-ounce) cans black beans, undrained

1 quart chicken broth

1 tablespoon Cajun seasoning (purchased or recipe page 182)

2 teaspoons salt

2 teaspoons freshly ground black pepper

3 bay leaves

1 1/2 teaspoons minced fresh thyme

1 teaspoon ground cumin

1/2 teaspoon smoked paprika

1/2 cup diced green onion

For serving: 2 tablespoons minced fresh parsley and 2 tablespoons minced fresh cilantro

# FROG LEG SAUCE PIQUANTE

MAKES 4 SERVINGS

2 tablespoons canola oil

1 pound cleaned frog legs (approximately 10–12)

1 tablespoon all-purpose flour

1 cup diced onions

¼ cup diced bell peppers

¼ cup diced celery

2 cloves garlic, minced

1 teaspoon salt

½ teaspoon cayenne pepper

3 cups red tomatoes, skinned, seeded, and chopped

1 bay leaf

1 teaspoon Cajun hot sauce

½ teaspoon dried thyme

2 tablespoons chopped parsley, divided

1 tablespoon freshly squeezed lemon juice

For serving: hot cooked rice (recipe page 166)

"Gigging" for frogs is a popular nighttime activity in Louisiana's marshes, crawfish ponds, and rice fields. In Baton Rouge, it's relatively easy to find frog legs pot-ready in area grocery stores. The frog leg industry is big around the southwest Louisiana town of Rayne, which at one time was the world's largest shipper of edible frogs.

**1.** Heat canola oil in a large skillet over the medium-high heat of a propane burner or stove. Add the frog legs and brown lightly on both sides, 2 to 3 minutes. Transfer the frog legs to a platter and set aside.

**2.** Add flour to the hot oil. Make a medium brown roux by stirring constantly for 4 to 5 minutes, until the color of a brown paper bag.

**3.** Add onions, bell peppers, celery, garlic, salt, and cayenne. Sauté until vegetables are wilted, about 5 minutes. Add the tomatoes, bay leaf, hot sauce, and thyme. When the mixture begins to bubble, reduce the heat to medium. Simmer, uncovered, 25 to 30 minutes. Stir occasionally to keep from sticking.

**4.** Lay the frog legs in the sauce and cook 3 to 4 minutes, basting occasionally. Taste and add more salt or hot sauce as needed. Stir in 1 tablespoon parsley and the lemon juice. Remove the bay leaves and serve frog legs and sauce over rice. Garnish with remaining parsley.

# PRODUCE

Okay, so I'm a meat kind of guy. But lately I find myself grilling more and more vegetables and cooking more grains. One reason is that the people closest to me insist on it, as do the clients who hire me to cater events. An even more important influence, however, is that the national focus on local eating has prompted farmers to raise interesting produce, which gives us consumers and professional cooks easier access to them.

I buy fruit, vegetables, and grains from many different vendors. On Saturday mornings, you can often find me in downtown Baton Rouge at the Red Stick Farmers' Market, which is jam-packed with well-stocked booths. When I cook for large parties, I need lots of everything, so that's when I buy directly from the farmer, usually from places like Fullness Organic Farm in Baton Rouge or Inglewood Farm in Alexandria.

It's important to mention that agriculture is a vital part of the Louisiana economy. There are close to thirty thousand farms in this state and over eight million acres of farmland. Away from our cities and swamps lie patchworks of cultivated fields stretching all the way to the horizon. In those well-tended fields grow our top commercial crops, which are sugarcane, soybeans, feed corn, and rice.

We eat a lot of rice in Louisiana, and that's because this grain is an extremely important commercial crop in the southwestern part of the state. We've been growing rice since the early 1700s. At first on a small scale, rice became big business in the late 1800s, when farmers realized that the wet, flat fields of the warm Acadiana prairie were ideal for nurturing it. Most farmers here plant long-grain rice, but they also grow medium- and short-grain. An expanding number are experimenting with jasmine varieties, and some are even taking the financial plunge and raising it organically.

When it comes to common vegetables, the state's "official vegetable" is the sweet potato. Sweet potatoes are at their tastiest around Thanksgiving time, when growers typically ship their "cured" product, potatoes that have been

**Jay with host Ted Allen on**
*Chopped Gold Medal Games.*

stored long enough to develop optimum sweetness and a soft, moist texture. And even though sweet potatoes are often called yams, the two tubers are not related. This was a marketing ploy established in the 1960s to distinguish Louisiana sweet potatoes from the less-sweet types grown on the East Coast.

Not to be outdone, the Creole tomato is Louisiana's "official state vegetable plant." Although there is a variety called "Creole," the Creole tomatoes so prized around here are any variety grown in the nutrient-rich alluvial soils of the southern parishes that line the Mississippi River, particularly in St. Bernard and Plaquemines parishes. Historically, Creoles are medium to large. They're extremely flavorful red tomatoes that are vine-ripened, and therefore easily perishable. In season I eat and cook with all the Creole tomatoes I can; you can't compare their taste to hothouse supermarket varieties.

Our state also has large commercial pecan, honey, and citrus industries. Fruits with the highest production are strawberries (our "state fruit"), peaches, and melons. Most large home gardens grow cantaloupe and watermelons. My favorite watermelons come from Washington Parish, which borders Mississippi in the southeastern part of the state, and where acidic sandy loam assures consistent sweetness.

Fortunately, many things grow well here, and I always try to buy as close to home as possible. Produce that's only a day or so old has such a crisp texture and vibrant taste that even the most unsophisticated palate can tell the difference. In Louisiana's mild climate, we're fortunate to be able to grow fruit and vegetables year-round. Spring is the time to pick strawberries, cabbages, leeks, lettuces, and onions. Summer is best for blueberries, blackberries, potatoes, tomatoes, okra, squash, eggplant, peaches, purple-hull peas, pole beans, and one of my favorites, figs. In the fall, we harvest persimmons and we plant greens, such as collards, lettuce, and mustard greens, which typically brave through the winter. The colder months also bring some of the sweetest, juiciest citrus you'll ever taste. Some of the easiest to find in markets are grapefruit, lemons, limes, kumquats, and several varieties of oranges. A couple of the more popular home citrus trees are Meyer lemons and the easy-to-peel satsuma.

## Falafel Flop

In a way, beans may have played a big role in helping me get chosen to be on the 2015 season of Food Network's reality show *Food Network Star.* This came about after what happened in August 2014, when I made my first Food Network appearance competing on *Cutthroat Kitchen,* hosted by the culinary celebrity Alton Brown. For each one-hour episode of *Cutthroat,* four chefs essentially sabotage each other while they're preparing their own dish. For the first round, we had to make minestrone, the Italian tomato-based meat-and-vegetable soup. I had to cook mine in a glass pitcher–style coffeepot. I could feel the pressure, but I worked through it, and I luckily advanced to the second round.

That second round had us making falafel, a chickpea fritter, a dish foreign to traditional Cajun cooking and something I'd only eaten a few times. To make things more challenging, I had to fish the dish's main ingredient, chickpeas, out of previously made minestrone, the whole while holding hands with another chef. Undaunted, I deftly used a food processor to grind my chickpeas with bread. With my one free hand, I rolled up my seasoned balls, tossed them into hot oil, and left them frying. By the time I got back to the fryer, dragging the chef I had to hold hands with, I found only over-fried shards of blown-up falafel. I knew I was toast. Regardless, I was determined not to give up, and I plated my falafel fragments, topped them with a creamy cucumber yogurt mint sauce, and proudly presented my dish for judging.

The judge, Chef Antonia Lofaso, took one look and asked, "What is this?" I replied, "I'm from Louisiana, and I love cracklins. This is falafel cracklins. Crunchy bits of falafel with a cucumber yogurt mint sauce." Right after that, I was eliminated. But instead of crumbling like my falafel, I had made a joke. And Antonio sang my praises for storytelling and trying to connect the dots rather than looking totally dejected. Some losing contestants get angry, or even beat themselves up, but I blithely laughed my falafel failure off. I'll probably never know for sure, but I like to believe that my smooth reaction to this catastrophe caught the eye of the producers at *Food Network Star.*

Jay's Trophy Case: In 2016, Baton Rouge's *225 Magazine* awarded Jay with its annual "Best of 225 Awards" for "best local celebrity" and "best media personality," categories that pit him against local radio and television newscasters. In 2017, Jay won a BRAG (Baton Rouge Area's Greatest) award from *Dig Magazine* for "greatest radio host." That same year, he also won *225*'s "best podcast" award. In 2018, he won for "best local blogger" in "Best of 225," and he also won *Dig*'s honor as "greatest local celebrity." In 2019, in his restaurant's first year of eligibility, Jay's Gov't Taco took home "best tacos at a local restaurant."

# GRILLED ASPARAGUS

MAKES 6 SERVINGS

2 bunches fresh asparagus, trimmed, woody ends removed

3 tablespoons olive oil

Kosher salt and freshly ground black pepper

Juice of 1 lemon

**If your asparagus are thin, go with a shorter cooking time.**

**1.** Prepare a grill or grill pan for medium-high heat. On a tray or in a baking pan, roll the dry asparagus spears around in the olive oil. Lightly season with salt and pepper and toss to mix.

**2.** Grill one side of asparagus over direct heat 3–4 minutes. Flip asparagus over and grill an additional 3–4 minutes. Place hot asparagus in a serving dish and toss with the lemon juice. Serve warm.

# STEWED OKRA WITH TOMATOES

MAKES 12 SERVINGS

1 pound fresh okra, or 1 pound sliced frozen okra

5 slices bacon

1 large onion, diced

3 cloves garlic, minced

1 jalapeño pepper, in small dice

2 pounds San Marzano or regular plum tomatoes, seeded and diced

2 teaspoons Creole seasoning (purchased or recipe page 182)

**Okra is one of those vegetables almost everyone in south Louisiana grew up with, and they usually love it or they hate it because of the vegetable's large seeds and slippery texture. In my case, okra rocks.**

**1.** For fresh okra, trim off stems and discard. Cut pods into $1/2$-inch slices. Set aside. Set a cast-iron pot of your choosing over the medium-high heat of a propane burner or your stove and render bacon until crisp. Leaving in the fat, remove bacon and set aside.

**2.** To the fat in the pot, add onion, garlic, and jalapeño. Sauté until soft, about 7 minutes. Stir in okra, tomatoes, and Creole seasoning. Cook over medium heat, uncovered, and stirring occasionally, until okra is tender, about 20–30 minutes. Serve warm.

# SMOKED CREOLE TOMATO SOUP

MAKES 4-6 SERVINGS

**1.** Prepare a smoker with wood chips for 250°F cooking. Season the outsides of the whole tomatoes with 1 tablespoon olive oil, salt, and pepper. Smoke them directly on a smoker rack until soft, about 30–40 minutes.

**2.** While tomatoes are smoking, in a large, heavy saucepan sauté onion and garlic in remaining 2 tablespoons olive oil until soft, about 6 minutes. Season with red pepper flakes, barbecue rub, and oregano.

**3.** Add smoked tomatoes to the onion mixture and simmer 15 minutes. Puree in a blender until smooth. To serve, pour into individual bowls and top with chopped basil.

Wood chips for smoking, soaked in water 30 minutes

2 pounds Creole tomatoes (about 8 small or 6 medium tomatoes)

3 tablespoons extra virgin olive oil, divided

Salt and freshly ground black pepper

1 small yellow onion, diced

2 cloves garlic, minced

1 teaspoon red pepper flakes

1 teaspoon Jay D's Spicy & Sweet Barbecue Rub (purchased or recipe page 183, or your favorite commercial brand)

1 teaspoon dried oregano

For serving: 2 tablespoons chopped purple basil

# GOCHUJANG EGGPLANT

MAKES 6 SERVINGS

**Gochujang Sauce:**

3 cups water, plus 3 tablespoons

1/2 cup low-sodium soy sauce

1/2 cup white sugar

1/3 cup minced fresh ginger

1/4 cup gochujang red chili paste

2 tablespoons sriracha sauce

2 tablespoons sesame seeds

1 tablespoon fish sauce

1 1/2 teaspoons garlic powder

1 1/2 teaspoons onion powder

1 1/2 teaspoons minced garlic

3 tablespoons water

2 tablespoons cornstarch

**Eggplant:**

2 medium purple eggplants, peeled

1 tablespoon extra virgin olive oil

1 teaspoon salt

1/2 teaspoon ground black pepper

For serving: 1 cup chopped peanuts and 5 green onions, thinly sliced

Eggplants grow well in the summer in Louisiana. Since this beautiful vegetable's flesh is bland, it pairs well with heavily seasoned sauces. Gochujang is a Korean fermented red chili paste that's hot and a little sweet. The heat comes from gochugaru, Korean red chili pepper powder. The hint of sweetness also comes from this particular variety of chili pepper, as well as from glutinous rice starch.

**1.** To make the sauce, combine all sauce ingredients except the 3 tablespoons water and cornstarch in a saucepan and simmer 15 minutes. Puree in a blender until smooth. Return to the saucepan and bring back to a simmer. Mix together remaining 3 tablespoons water and cornstarch to make a slurry. Whisking constantly, add slurry to the sauce. Let simmer 2 minutes, stirring occasionally, and remove from heat.

**2.** Cut eggplant into 2-inch-long logs, each about 1/2 inch thick. In a sauté skillet set over the medium-high heat of a propane burner or your stove, heat olive oil and sauté eggplant until soft but al dente. Sprinkle with salt and black pepper while cooking. Toss cooked eggplant in as much Gochujang sauce as you like. Garnish with chopped peanuts and sliced green onion. Serve warm.

# SMOKY ROASTED CARROTS AND BRUSSELS SPROUTS

MAKES 6 SERVINGS

Preheat a covered grill to medium-high with soaked wood chips, or an indoor oven to 425°F. Combine all ingredients in a large bowl and toss vegetables until well coated with seasoning. Spread a large sheet of heavy-duty aluminum foil on top of the grill, and arrange vegetables on foil in one layer. For oven baking, arrange vegetables on sheet pans. Close grill cover and roast until vegetables are tender, about 30 minutes. Should take about the same amount of time in an oven. Serve warm or at room temperature.

Wood chips for smoking, soaked 30 minutes

12 medium carrots, in ½-inch slices

1 pound Brussels sprouts, cut in half lengthwise

2 tablespoons olive oil

2 tablespoons Jay D's Spicy & Sweet Barbecue Rub (purchased or recipe page 183, or your favorite commercial brand)

# WHOLE ROASTED CAULIFLOWER

MAKES 4–6 SERVINGS

1 large head cauliflower

¼ cup Jay D's Louisiana Molasses Mustard (purchased or recipe page 184)

1 tablespoon garlic olive oil

Salt and ground black pepper to taste

**1.** Preheat one side of a covered grill to medium-high, or an oven to 375°F. Remove the outer leaves of the cauliflower. Trim the stem flush with the bottom of the cauliflower so that it sits flat. Mix together the molasses mustard and olive oil and gently brush on the outside of the cauliflower. Season with salt and pepper.

**2.** Roast the cauliflower in a cast-iron skillet over covered indirect grill heat or in the oven until you can easily pierce it with a knife, about 1 hour. Cool slightly and cut into small florets. Serve warm.

# BRAISED GREENS

MAKES 12 SERVINGS

Combine all ingredients in a cast-iron pot over the medium-high heat of a propane burner or stove. Bring to a boil, then reduce to a simmer. Cook, covered, stirring occasionally, until greens are extremely tender, about 45 minutes to 1 hour. Serve as a side dish or in bowls with the pot likker, the cooking juices, for dipping cornbread.

4 bunches fresh mustard, collard, or turnip greens, washed thoroughly, stemmed, and roughly chopped

1 smoked ham hock

2 large onions, in small dice

8 cloves garlic, minced

2 cups chicken broth

1/2 cup white vinegar

1/4 cup olive oil

1 1/2 tablespoons cane syrup

1 tablespoon Cajun seasoning (purchased or recipe page 182)

1 tablespoon Louisiana-style hot sauce

For serving: Cornbread (recipe page 21)

# PICKLED RED ONIONS

MAKES ABOUT 2 PINTS (BEGIN A DAY AHEAD)

**Even though I don't eat regular cucumber pickles, I do like other pickled vegetables, such as this tangy onion condiment, which adds a vibrant punch to grilled meats and sandwiches.**

**1.** Make a brine in a medium bowl by mixing together vinegar, water, and sugar. Stir until sugar is dissolved.

**2.** Add onions to the bowl, or cover onions completely with brine in glass pint jars. Cover bowl or jars tightly, and allow onions to pickle overnight in the refrigerator.

3 cups rice vinegar

1 cup water

1/2 cup sugar

2 small red onions, thinly shaved

# SMOKED SWEET CORN WITH BARBECUE BUTTER

MAKES 4 SERVINGS

Wood chips for smoking, soaked in water 30 minutes

4 ears of fresh sweet corn, with husks and silk

2 tablespoons Barbecue Compound Butter (recipe page 181)

¼ cup crumbled queso fresco or feta cheese

**1.** Prepare a covered grill or smoker with wood chips to medium-low heat, or set an oven to 275°F. Place whole ears of corn, husks and all, directly on the grates. Grill, cover closed, or bake in a pan until soft, about 1 hour.

**2.** Remove the husks and silk from the corn and discard. Rub the corn ears with the compound butter; then sprinkle on the cheese. Serve warm.

Corn maque choux.

# GRILLED MAQUE CHOUX

MAKES 4 SERVINGS

Early Cajuns learned how to make this stewed corn, pronounced mock-shoe, from Native Americans indigenous to south Louisiana. That was sometime in the 1700s, and maque choux is still a staple on our tables.

**1.** Prepare a grill for medium heat. Shuck the corn and remove the silk. Slather the ears with the olive oil and sprinkle with salt and black pepper. Grill, rotating the ears regularly, so that they char but don't scorch. Should take 10–15 minutes.

**2.** When corn is cool enough to handle, use a large knife to cut the kernels off the cobs. "Milk" the cobs by using the back of the knife to scrape off any liquid. Set the kernels and corn milk aside. Heat a large heavy-bottomed saucepan over the medium-high heat of a propane burner or stove. Add canola oil, along with the onion, bell pepper, celery, garlic, and jalapeño. Sauté until the onions are sweated, 10–12 minutes.

**3.** Add the wine and simmer until the wine has evaporated, about 5 minutes. Stir in the bay leaf, red pepper flakes, paprika, thyme, cayenne, chili powder, and as much salt and pepper as you like. Add the corn and its milk to the Dutch oven. Add the cream and butter, stir, and bring to a simmer. Cook until thickened, when it has a slight creamed-corn consistency, 5–7 minutes. Remove the bay leaves. Pour into a serving bowl, sprinkle on the green onion, and serve hot.

3 large ears corn

2 tablespoons olive oil

Kosher salt and freshly ground black pepper

1 tablespoon canola oil

1 cup finely chopped onion

1/2 cup chopped red bell pepper

1 stalk celery, diced

1 clove garlic, minced

1 teaspoon minced jalapeño pepper

1/2 cup white wine

1 dried bay leaf

1/2 teaspoon red pepper flakes

1/4 teaspoon paprika

1/4 teaspoon dried thyme

1/4 teaspoon cayenne pepper

1/4 teaspoon chili powder

3/4 cup heavy whipping cream

2 tablespoons unsalted butter

For serving: green onion chopped on the bias

# BLACK-EYED PEAS

MAKES 4 SERVINGS (BEGIN A DAY AHEAD)

½ pound dried black-eyed peas

Water

½ pound heavily smoked ham, chopped into ¼-inch cubes (optional)

2 tablespoons olive oil

1 medium onion, diced

2 stalks celery, diced

1 medium green bell pepper, seeded and diced

1 teaspoon minced fresh jalapeño pepper

3 cloves garlic, minced

½ cup chicken broth

2 bay leaves

1 teaspoon kosher salt

½ teaspoon ground black pepper

¼ cup finely chopped green onion

**1.** Rinse peas and place in a large bowl. Cover by 2 inches water and let stand overnight.

**2.** The next day, to a Dutch oven, add the ham and olive oil. Over the medium-high heat of a propane burner or your stove, sauté ham until brown. Remove and set aside. Add the onion, celery, bell pepper, and jalapeño. Sauté until onion is translucent, about 6 minutes. Add the garlic and sauté 30 seconds. Add the broth and scrape up the browned bits from the bottom of the pan.

**3.** Drain the peas, add them to the pot, and add enough water to cover by 1 inch. Add the bay leaves, salt, and black pepper. Bring to a boil, reduce heat to a bare simmer, cover, and cook until beans are tender, about 1½ hours. Remove cover and simmer, stirring occasionally, until peas turn creamy, about 15–20 more minutes. Remove the bay leaves, stir in the green onion, and serve warm.

# RED BEANS AND RICE BALLS

MAKES 2 TO 3 DOZEN GOLF BALL–SIZED HORS D'OEUVRES
(BEGIN AT LEAST A DAY AHEAD)

Even though they're supposed to be a starter, you can make a meal of these crispy babies. If you don't have leftover red beans and you start from scratch, begin this recipe two days ahead. If you already have cooked beans, you'll need them to set up in the refrigerator overnight.

1. Make the Red Beans and Rice with Pork Sausage recipe (page 60), but don't include the sausage. Refrigerate the cooked beans overnight.

2. The next day, cook rice according to instructions on page 166. Fold cooked rice into the cold red bean mixture. Refrigerate at least 2 hours.

3. When ready to fry, make an egg wash by whisking together the eggs and milk. Place flour in a shallow pan. In another shallow pan, combine breading mix and breadcrumbs.

4. In a cast-iron Dutch oven, heat 2 inches vegetable oil over a propane burner or on your stove to 350°F. Form the chilled red bean and rice mixture into golf ball–sized balls. Roll each ball in flour, then in egg wash, and then in breadcrumb mixture. Place small batches into hot oil. Fry until golden brown, about 3–4 minutes. Drain on paper towels. Serve hot with Barbecue Aioli and Pickled Red Onions.

1 recipe Red Beans and Rice, without the sausage (from recipe page 60)

3 cups raw medium-grain rice

6 large eggs

1 cup milk

1 cup all-purpose flour

1 cup seasoned seafood breading mix (such as Slap Ya Mama brand Cajun Fish Fry or Zatarain's)

1 cup panko breadcrumbs

Vegetable oil for frying

For serving: Barbecue Aioli (recipe page 185) and Pickled Red Onions (recipe page 155)

# GERMAN-STYLE POTATO SALAD

MAKES 4 SERVINGS

6 slices bacon

1 pound (2 medium) Yukon Gold potatoes, peeled

Kosher salt to taste

2 tablespoons apple cider vinegar

1 tablespoon whole grain Creole mustard

½ teaspoon ground black pepper

1 tomato, seeded and diced

4 green onions, chopped

4 teaspoons chopped parsley

4 teaspoons sliced chives

**1.** Preheat a covered grill for indirect heat on high, approximately 400°F, or set your oven to the same temperature. Meanwhile, in a large cast-iron skillet, cook bacon on both sides until really crispy, 5–10 minutes. Reserving bacon fat, remove bacon from skillet and dry on paper towels. When cool, crumble bacon and set aside.

**2.** Cut potatoes into 1½-inch chunks. Toss them in the skillet in the rendered bacon fat with a few pinches of salt. Roast potatoes in the skillet on the cool side of the covered grill or in the oven 10 minutes, then turn them over. Cook until fork tender and golden brown, 5 to 10 more minutes.

**3.** Toss potatoes with vinegar, mustard, and black pepper. Stir in bacon bits, tomato, green onion, and parsley. Top with chives and serve warm.

# MOLASSES MUSTARD POTATO SALAD

MAKES 4 SERVINGS

**1.** In a large pot set over a propane burner or your stove, cover potatoes by 2 inches water and add ½ teaspoon salt. Bring to a boil, lower to a simmer, and cook until potatoes are tender but still firm, about 15 minutes. Drain and cool. Coarsely chop the potatoes, if desired.

**2.** In a large bowl, combine the mayonnaise, mustard, red onion, green onion, parsley, and syrup. Toss in the potatoes, carefully coating all surfaces. Refrigerate until chilled through and serve.

1½ pounds red potatoes, peeled and cut into 1-inch cubes

Water

Kosher salt

2 tablespoons mayonnaise

2 tablespoons Jay D's Louisiana Molasses Mustard (purchased or recipe page 184)

1 tablespoon diced red onion

1 tablespoon diced green onion

1 tablespoon finely chopped parsley

1½ teaspoons Steen's Cane Syrup (or substitute light molasses or maple syrup)

# SPICY HASSELBACK POTATOES WITH YOGURT DIPPING SAUCE

MAKES 4 SERVINGS

1 cup (2 sticks) unsalted butter

1 tablespoon, plus 1 cup Jay D's Spicy & Sweet Barbecue Rub (purchased or recipe page 183, or your favorite commercial brand)

8 medium-small potatoes (Yukon Gold, fingerlings, or red bliss)

2 tablespoons chopped green onion

For serving: Yogurt Dipping Sauce (recipe follows) and 2 tablespoons chopped green onion

**1.** Preheat a covered grill to medium-high or an oven to 425°F. In a small saucepan, melt the butter with 1 tablespoon barbecue rub.

**2.** Place a potato between the handles of 2 wooden spoons or 2 chopsticks. Using a sharp knife, make crosswise cuts in each potato, about $1/8$ inch apart. (The spoon handles prevent you from slicing the potato all the way through.) Repeat with remaining potatoes.

**3.** Place the potatoes in a large cast-iron skillet and pour the butter mixture between each potato slice. Bake on the indirect heat side of the covered grill or in the oven until golden brown and tender, about 55–60 minutes. To serve, garnish the hot potatoes with the green onion and serve alongside the Yogurt Dipping Sauce.

# YOGURT DIPPING SAUCE

MAKES 1 CUP

Aside from potatoes, this simple sauce is good with raw vegetables and fried chicken fingers.

Combine the yogurt and the molasses mustard in a bowl or jar. Cover and refrigerate up to 3 days.

1 cup Greek yogurt

3 tablespoons Jay D's Louisiana Molasses Mustard (purchased or recipe page 184)

Hasselback potatoes.

# ROASTED SWEET POTATOES

MAKES AS MANY AS YOU WANT

Whole sweet potatoes, washed and dried

When I was a youngster I became an expert at roasting sweet potatoes at my family's hunting campsites. I love sweet potatoes, and I think whole roasted ones are best eaten plain. If you want to jazz yours up, top it with Barbecue Compound Butter (recipe page 181) or Herb Butter (recipe page 68).

*In coals:* Make a charcoal fire and let the flames go out. Poke holes in the tops of sweet potatoes with a fork and wrap them in two layers of heavy-duty aluminum foil. Use tongs to bury potatoes in the coals, with more coals beneath them than on top. Rotate potatoes every 15 minutes and cook until extremely soft. Depending on size, this takes 1–1$\frac{1}{2}$ hours.

*On a grill or smoker:* Preheat a covered grill or smoker to medium, 350°F. Poke holes in the tops of sweet potatoes with a fork. Wrap them individually in aluminum foil and place on grill grates over indirect fire. Close the lid and cook 45 minutes. Pierce sweet potatoes with a skewer or fork to check for doneness. They should be extremely soft. Depending on size, they may take an additional 30–40 minutes.

*In the oven:* Preheat your oven to 375°F. Poke holes in the tops of sweet potatoes with a fork. Place them on a foil-lined sheet pan and put in the oven. If your potatoes have lots of natural sugar, their juice will briskly ooze out of the fork holes in about 1–1$\frac{1}{2}$ hours, and they're done. If no juice appears by then, pierce with a fork to see if they're cooked. They should be extremely soft.

# PEAR AND HAVARTI GRILLED CHEESE SANDWICHES

MAKES 2 SERVINGS

**This sandwich is quick and easy, yet sophisticated.**

**1.** Spread one side of each bread slice with Molasses Mustard. Divide cheese evenly on top of all the bread slices. Divide pear slices between 2 bread slices, and top those with remaining cheese-covered bread.

**2.** Heat a large sauté pan over medium-high heat on a grill or on your stove. Add the butter and cook each side of sandwiches until bread is golden-brown and cheese is melted. Immediately slice sandwiches in half and serve.

4 slices sourdough bread

2 tablespoons Jay D's Louisiana Molasses Mustard (purchased or recipe page 184)

8 ounces Havarti cheese, sliced

1 fresh, ripe pear, sliced into thin strips

2 tablespoons unsalted butter, softened

# COOKED WHITE RICE

MAKES 3 CUPS

2 cups water

1 teaspoon kosher salt

1 cup raw long-grain white rice

All my life I've watched various Cajun grandmothers cook rice without measuring anything, and it turns out perfect every time. Me, I need a recipe.

**1.** In a medium saucepan set over the medium-high heat of a propane burner or your stove, bring water and salt to a boil. Stir in rice, bring back to a boil, then lower to a bare simmer. Cover tightly and cook until rice has absorbed all the liquid and is just tender, about 20 minutes.

**2.** Remove pot from the heat. Let sit, covered tightly, for 10 minutes. (Don't raise the lid during those 10 minutes.) Fluff rice with a fork and serve.

# COOKED BROWN RICE

MAKES 3 CUPS

2½ cups water

1 teaspoon kosher salt

1 cup raw long-grain brown rice

**1.** Put all ingredients into a medium saucepan and bring to a boil over the medium-high heat of a propane burner or your stove. Lower to a bare simmer and cover tightly. Cook until rice is tender and the liquid is absorbed, about 40–50 minutes.

**2.** Remove pot from the heat. Let sit, covered tightly, for 15 minutes. (Don't raise the lid during those 15 minutes.) Fluff rice with a fork and serve.

# SPREADING THE WORD

9

I guess you could say I'm on a quest to bring my passion for Cajun food to the entire universe. I mostly do that by traveling, and wherever I land I usually cook. I particularly like demonstrating Louisiana recipes, and I'll teach the arts of smothering, frying, and grilling to anyone who'll listen. Be it a traditional po'boy, gumbo, or étouffée, or a modern take on bisque, or something made with rice, I'm ready to show the uninitiated how it's done.

When I'm teaching, a vital point I stress is that no dish will taste right if the flavors aren't built in. Proper seasoning is especially important when preparing complex dishes such as étouffée or gumbo, when it's essential to have a knowledge of Cajun Cooking 101: To make that all-important first layer of flavor, sauté the "Cajun trinity" of onion, bell pepper, and celery, which adds magical depth to savory dishes. (The trinity is so essential to south Louisiana cooking that almost any grocery store sells it pre-chopped and frozen.)

Another important flavor-enhancement step is to season correctly with salt and pepper. To taste right, food needs salt, even desserts, so unless you have a medical condition, don't omit salt in a recipe. And don't make the mistake that many people make, that Cajun food should be fiery hot. Savory Louisiana dishes certainly include some pepper, but fiery heat should not be the primary flavor. My grandmothers had a knack for throwing in just the right amount of black pepper and cayenne pepper, which are common in savory Cajun cooking. Their food was never too spicy.

Today's tastes still call for those salt-and-pepper basics, but we've also learned to use a wider variety of seasonings. In the 1970s, an Opelousas drug salesman named Tony Chachere invented his "Original Creole Seasoning," a salt-based concoction of cayenne, black pepper, chili powder, garlic powder, and a few secret spices. Tony's, as the salt-based spice mixture is commonly called, is still a best seller. When Chef Paul Prudhomme introduced Cajun food to the world in the 1980s, many of his recipes included separate seasoning-mix blends. It was at this time that premixed Cajun spice blends became kitchen staples.

Many Cajun spice blends include dried herbs. I'm really into herbs, and I like to use fresh thyme, my favorite, as well as bay leaf and oregano. Parsley and green onion are also standards in my repertoire. To maximize their flavor, I typically add these herbs at the end of the cooking time, or I use them for garnish. I don't cook too much with the one herb distinctly associated with Louisiana, filé. Filé was created by the Choctaws, and it's a powder ground from the dried leaf of the sassafras tree. Its flavor reminds me of an earthy root beer, and for centuries it's been used as a gumbo thickener. I've tried experimenting with filé in recipes other than gumbo, but it just doesn't seem to add anything that a little lemon or other herbs couldn't. A bottle of filé is, however, a standard condiment when I serve gumbo.

The final way to get the flavor right is to taste and make adjustments throughout the cooking process. My grandmothers, like so many fine home cooks, constantly dipped their tasting spoons into the pot. Even if you're following a good recipe, you never know how your dish will end up tasting, so it's always best to try a nibble and not be disappointed.

I feel I've accomplished something if I can get a novice cook to learn to taste constantly and get the hang of cooking with these basic seasoning techniques. Cajun cooking isn't hard. It just has a few rules that need to be followed.

## Jay D's Louisiana Flavors

Another way I spread the good word about what we eat in Louisiana is through my commercial line of seasonings. After a few years of food blogging and hosting my radio show, I was earning some revenue from advertisers, including from my major sponsor, the fantastic folks at Calandro's Supermarket, but I really had nothing tangible to sell. To solve that problem, I started thinking about creating a line of food products made with Louisiana ingredients. The condiments I chose to sell commercially are based on mixes I'd been making in big batches and turning to for years. Most of the time when I'm cooking I don't have time to measure out a laundry list of seasoning and sauce ingredients, and all along I've been using my premixed blends to make things easy.

In 2014, I commercially launched my Jay D's Louisiana Barbecue Sauce, which I make in small batches at the Panola Pepper Company in Lake Providence, Louisiana. It's spicy and slightly sweet, and is based on tomato, mustard, apple cider vinegar, and Louisiana cane syrup. Then came my appearance on

*An assortment of Jay D's products.*

*Food Network Star* and my impromptu preparation of a dipping sauce for my Big Jay's Cajun Burger with Potato Chips. The burger got a huge thumbs-up, as did the sauce, which was a blend of mustard, hot sauce, and molasses. Later that year, I bottled that recipe as Jay D's Louisiana Molasses Mustard. My latest commercial condiment is Jay D's Spicy & Sweet Barbecue Rub. This recipe is based on one I've used for years in competition barbecue, and it's a blend of spices that includes Louisiana's favorite hot pepper, cayenne, as well as smoked paprika and traditional Louisiana spices like onion and garlic.

## Seasoning with Booze

You've probably figured out that I enjoy sipping the occasional alcoholic beverage. Over the years, I've also learned that cooking with beer, wine, and spirts enhances the flavor of many dishes. My curiosity about cooking with booze started in high school, when (behind my parents' backs) I experimented with marinating wild quail in whiskey. Later, I seriously researched alcohol's effect

**Jay grilling in Las Terrenas, Dominican Republic.**

on both savories and sweets. I even filled a corkboard with color-coded index cards scribbled with ideas for pairing foods with beer, wine, distilled spirits, and liqueurs.

During that painstaking process I learned that local craft beer makes gumbo richer. Vodka makes a pie crust flakier, and a few tablespoons of rum keeps sorbet from freezing rock hard. I finally figured out that wine, in particular, enhances flavors, and about 20 percent of my recipes call for it.

I like drinking and cooking with wine so much that in 2015 I started bottling my own label, Jay D's Blanc du Bois. It all started on one of my gastronomic adventures, when I stumbled upon Landry Vineyards in the northern part of the state, in West Monroe, Louisiana. There, winemaker Jeff Landry grows spectacular vines of Blanc du Bois, a hybrid grape created to withstand Pierce's Disease, the bacterial infection that destroys cool-weather grapes in the humid South. Jeff and I collaborated to come up with a handcrafted white wine that boasts crisp fruit forward. With flavors of peach and pear and a sultry honeysuckle aroma, this wine compliments Louisiana's highly seasoned cuisine. But if you're serving something spicy like sauce picante and you don't have a bottle of my wine around, uncork any still or bubbly white or rosé. Dry or sweet whites and pinks are naturally low in tannins, and they tend to balance strong flavors. That means they'll enhance, not compete with, the complex flavors of Cajun food.

## Creating Jobs through Coffee

One of my best friends, Caroline Payne, is a political science professor at Lycoming College in Pennsylvania, where she focuses on international government and civil conflict in developing nations. Before she accepted this position, she spent much of her time nudging me through my coursework in grad school at LSU. (Once she even nursed me through a hangover.) After college, when I taught high school and coached the school's baseball team, Caroline volunteered to tutor my Cuban-born players.

Nowadays, Caroline leads her students on expeditions in the developing world where they hope to help communities alleviate poverty. One of her primary destinations is El Naranjito, a remote community in the mountains of central Dominican Republic, where coffee growing is pretty much the only means of revenue. Unfortunately, the coffee farmers in this area have two factors going against them: Only 3 to 5 percent of Dominican-grown coffee is exported, so there's no reason to strive for high quality, which would give them

**Jay in El Naranjito with friend and business partner Caroline Payne.**

the chance to sell to the global specialty-grade coffee market. The second hindrance is the region's isolation, which keeps farmers beholden to middlemen who pay them as little as five to eight cents per pound. Both road-blocks make these coffee farmers some of the poorest in the world.

I'd been following the progress of Caroline's mission, and a few years ago, I proposed a collaboration: that she work with the farmers to supply high-quality coffee beans, and that I bring some of the coffee beans that she imports to Louisiana and roast them here as part of my product line. She was more excited than I was to grow the project. I then teamed up with Chris Peneguy and Stevie Guillory from Baton Rouge's Cafeciteaux Specialty Coffee Roasters and did some roasting and testing with the El Naranjito coffee beans. What we wound up with is an incredibly rich coffee with flavors of milk chocolate, fig, and nutmeg. Even though many folks here like their coffee dark, we decided that a medium roast would treat this coffee with the respect it deserves. It certainly tasted good to us, and we thought that aficionados would appreciate its earthy nuances.

I named my product Jay D's Single Origin Coffee, and I'm happy to say that sales are doing great. In the meantime, Caroline is working with the El Naranjito community to improve their agricultural and processing techniques, including using environmentally safe practices that will possibly allow them to obtain Organic Certification. Her efforts have resulted in the farmers' earnings increasing to around two dollars a pound. I do my part by buying their green coffee beans through direct trade. I roast them here in Baton Rouge and package Jay D's Single Origin Coffee as whole beans that sell in local markets and online. Money from every bag sold goes back to Lycoming College, which they use to help El Naranjito farmers plant trees and learn about water and soil management. This money also sends American students to the Dominican Republic, where they learn how to grow coffee responsibly.

## Keep on Keepin' On

Ten years ago, if you had asked me my goal, I would have said it was to have my own show on the Travel Channel. When the *Baton Rouge Business Report* named me to their 2011 class of Forty Under 40, they asked that if I could have any job other than my own, what would it be? I responded, "Anthony Bourdain's job." Bourdain's passing a few years later left me seriously bummed. When I was beginning my career in food-and-beverage journalism, this giant in the culinary industry was a huge inspiration. I admired his approach to different cultures and his open-mindedness, and I've always tried to adapt those attitudes to my own globe-trotting.

Bourdain left us way too soon, but life does go on. I'm thirty-eight now. Maybe I'll be walking in his celebrity footsteps by my mid-forties. Until then, I have plenty of things to keep me busy. I'm happy working in my restaurant and with my catering business, which is almost always booked with corporate parties and pop-ups. I'm amazed at the number of pop-ups that are hosted in our area. My catering calendar is full of them, with clients who want me to cook at breweries, distilleries, festivals, bars, retail stores, and commercial offices. We've even done one underneath the I-10 Mississippi River Bridge. I'm honored to be one of Baton Rouge's go-to guys for hosting these increasingly popular events, and my catering team and I always look forward to the excitement of cooking somewhere different.

On the regular media front, I have my radio show and the weekly cooking demo, *Cookin' Louisiane,* on Fox 44 TV. And I still work with my video-producer friend, Tommy Talley. We even formed a joint venture called Small Batch Media, which is a culinary communications company that helps clients with video, branding, menu consultation, and design. It also helps to have these services at my fingertips to amp visibility for my personal corporation, Bite and Booze, my product line, Hug Jay D, and my restaurant, Gov't Taco.

When I'm not behind a radio microphone or in front of a TV camera or a grill, I do something else I enjoy: I try to keep ahead of food trends. Early in my culinary media journey, I realized that if I was going to make a career out of talking about food, I needed to know everything there was about who was eating what. That learning curve involves seeing popular new dishes and techniques firsthand, so as much as I can, I travel to food destinations. From New York to California to Mexico to Central America and to Europe and India, I've seen as much as I can, and there's so much more to see. And when I get where I'm going, I fall back on a technique I was taught while enrolled in the humanities at LSU: I study people and culture through the lens of beverage and food.

Learning from the masters is always helpful, and it was particularly so when I was setting the menu for my restaurant. Gov't Taco officially opened in May 2018, and in July 2019 we won the "Best of 225" (magazine) award for Best Tacos at a Local Restaurant. I knew that I wanted to deliver modern flavor profiles that jump out at you, and that attention-grabbing ingredients present

**Raise a glass.**

well when served on a tortilla. The tortilla is the perfect vessel to bring forward amazing combinations of flavors and textures to create that perfect bite. At Gov't Taco we get to play around with whatever flavors we want in the form of a taco. A lot of them are inspired by my products, as well as traditional Louisiana and southern cuisine. But we also turn to international flavors, and we always use farm-fresh ingredients.

I also soak up a lot of knowledge just by listening to the guests I interview on my radio show and by reading and responding to comments on my blog. It is these same supporters who have made *Bite & Booze* a success. Without their interest and participation, I would not have had the opportunity to appear on numerous national television cooking shows. My fans gave me the confidence I needed to win cooking awards, start that line of sauces and condiments, create my own wine label, and even have my own brand of coffee.

But, of course, none of this would have happened if I hadn't lit up that first grill on campus and pretended that I knew what I was doing. My wonderful career began with the skills I learned as a college student cooking outdoors. Back then, I could have never imagined my occupation: relaxing under a tent while sipping a few brews and grilling, and then talking about it to anyone who'll listen. I couldn't ask for a better way to make a living.

The team at James Beard House.

Venison tenderloin.

Smothered fried catfish.

In 2016, Jay hosted an LSU tailgate party–themed dinner at the prestigious James Beard House in New York. The menu included Quail-Andouille Gumbo with Louisiana Rice, Crawfish Étouffée–Smothered Fried Catfish with Stone-Ground Grits and Mustard Greens, Blackened Red Snapper with Cajun Tasso-Corn Maque Choux and Jalapeño Relish, Venison Tenderloin with Chimichurri and Okra Three Ways, and Granny's Cinnamon Pecan Rolls. Each menu item was paired with a different beer, wine, or cocktail with Louisiana ties.

# TEXAS-STYLE FLOUR TORTILLAS

MAKES 12 SIX-INCH (OR 4 TWELVE-INCH) TORTILLAS

**1.** In a large mixing bowl, combine flour, salt, and baking powder. Grab the bowl with one hand and combine the dry ingredients with the other hand. Add the lard and use your same mixing hand to combine it with the flour mixture. While mixing, slowly add hot water (as hot as your hand can take). Slowly rotate the bowl and mix until the dough comes together and forms a ball, with little to no dough stuck to the the bowl.

**2.** Place dough ball on a hard surface and knead until smooth and elastic, about 5 minutes. Place dough back in the bowl and cover with a warm, damp towel. Allow to sit 20 minutes.

**3.** Divide the dough into twelve equal pieces. On a hard surface, roll each piece into small balls. Use a rolling pin or tortilla press to flatten the balls into thick, round 6-inch discs. Dust surfaces with flour as needed to keep from sticking.

**4.** When you're ready to cook, use a medium-high flame to heat an ungreased outdoor griddle, or use a large cast-iron skillet on your stove. Toss tortillas onto the hot griddle. The dough will rise and bubble as it cooks. Once bubbles form and hold for a few seconds, after about 30 seconds, flip the tortilla over and cook the other side. Should take another 30 seconds to cook completely. Remove from the griddle, and create the taco of your dreams.

2 cups all-purpose flour, plus additional for dusting

2 heaping teaspoons kosher salt

1½ teaspoons baking powder

½ cup pork lard (can substitute butter or shortening, but the flavor and texture won't be the same)

½ to 1 cup hot water

# COCONUT CHILI-CHOCOLATE TARTS

1 (16-ounce) bag almond flour

3/4 cup coconut oil, melted

1/2 cup honey

2 (14-ounce) cans coconut milk

1 1/2 teaspoons ancho chili powder

1 1/2 teaspoons pasilla chili powder

1 1/2 teaspoons smoked sea salt

1/4 teaspoon cayenne pepper, or to taste

24 ounces dark chocolate chips or chunks

**Yes, you can cook desserts on a grill. For this recipe, get a grill going on high heat (400°F). When it's time to "bake," do so over indirect heat. The filling can be cooked over a propane burner.**

**1.** Preheat a covered grill at high heat for indirect cooking or an oven to 400°F. In a stand mixer fitted with a paddle attachment, combine the almond flour, coconut oil, and honey on low speed until mixture becomes semi-clumpy. It should feel damp and moldable, similar to modeling clay.

**2.** Divide the mixture into 10 pieces and press each portion firmly onto bottom and up sides of 10 (6-inch) tart cups. Place the crust-lined tart cups on a sheet tray, and bake in the covered grill over indirect heat or in the oven until they rise a bit, look toasty, and the excess coconut oil bakes off, 18–20 minutes.

**3.** Meanwhile, make a ganache filling. In a saucepan set over the medium heat of a propane burner or your stove, bring the coconut milk to a simmer. Whisk in the ancho powder, pasilla powder, sea salt, and cayenne pepper. Place the chocolate in a large bowl. Pour the simmering coconut milk over the chocolate and whisk until melted. Set aside.

**4.** When tart shells are done, fill each evenly with the chocolate ganache. Let it firm up at room temperature or in the refrigerator for 1–2 hours. Serve at room temperature.

# PRETZEL BREAD PUDDING

MAKES 12 SERVINGS

After one of my catering company's cooking events we had a stack of pretzel buns leftover, so we decided to use it up in bread pudding. The finished dish was stunningly delicious, with a touch of saltiness that pairs well with the sweetness of the accompanying Pecan Rum Sauce.

**1.** Preheat a covered grill or your oven to 350°F. Use your hands to crumble pretzel buns into small pieces. Set aside.

**2.** In a 13×9-inch metal baking pan, mix together egg yolks, whole egg, and sugar until smooth. Stir in cream, vanilla extract, and cinnamon. With your hands, mix the custard and the crumbled pretzels together until you have the consistency of oatmeal.

**3.** Place the pan on the cool side of the grill and cover, or place in oven. Bake until the middle is set and the top is golden brown, about 30–45 minutes. Serve warm topped with Pecan Rum Sauce.

10 hot dog– or hamburger-sized pretzel buns

10 egg yolks

1 whole egg

1 cup sugar

3 cups heavy cream

1 tablespoon vanilla extract

1/2 tablespoon cinnamon

For serving: Pecan Rum Sauce (recipe follows)

# PECAN RUM SAUCE

MAKES ABOUT 1 1/2 CUPS

This sauce is also good on pound cake, French toast, and ice cream.

Over the medium heat of a propane burner or stove, combine sugar and butter in a heavy saucepan and cook until everything is melted. Stir in cream, rum, and cinnamon. When mixture comes to a simmer, add pecan pieces and simmer until thickened. Serve warm.

1 cup light brown sugar, packed

1/2 cup (1 stick) unsalted butter

1/2 cup heavy cream

1/4 cup dark rum

1/2 teaspoon ground cinnamon

1 cup pecan pieces

# GRANNY'S PECAN ROLLS

MAKES 16 ROLLS

Dough:

2½ cups all-purpose flour

¾ cup whole milk

⅓ cup canola oil

1 tablespoon sugar

2 teaspoons baking powder

1 teaspoon kosher salt

Filling:

4 tablespoons (½ stick) unsalted butter, melted

½ cup light brown sugar

2 tablespoons sugar

2 teaspoons cinnamon

½ cup chopped pecans

Praline Sauce:

1 cup heavy cream

1 cup light brown sugar

1 cup praline liqueur

**More than any other, this recipe takes me back to my childhood and the mouthwatering smells that came out of my grandmother's kitchen. These cinnamon rolls are so good that I made them when I cooked a "Tailgate Party" dinner at the James Beard House in New York in 2016.**

**1.** Preheat a grill or your oven to 350°F. Dump all the dough ingredients into a large mixing bowl and mix everything together with your hands. Remove to a hard surface lightly sprinkled with flour and knead until the dough is smooth, about 2 minutes. Roll the dough into a ball. Cover with a damp paper towel or plastic wrap and let rest 10 to 15 minutes.

**2.** On a lightly floured surface, roll out the dough into an 8-inch square, which should be approximately ⅛ to ¼-inch thick.

**3.** To make the filling, in a bowl, mix together the melted butter, brown sugar, sugar, and cinnamon. Spread the mixture evenly over the entire sheet of rolled dough. Sprinkle the chopped pecans evenly on top of the butter and sugar. Starting on one end, roll the dough jellyroll style to form a tight pinwheel log. Use a thin, sharp knife to slice the log into ½-inch thick rounds. Place the slices in a greased cast-iron Dutch oven and cover the pot. (For oven cooking, don't cover the pan.) Bake on the cool side of the covered, preheated grill or in the oven until golden, about 15 to 18 minutes.

**4.** To make the Praline Sauce, in a small saucepot set over medium heat, whisk together the cream, brown sugar, and praline liqueur. Bring to a simmer and cook until thick, about 10 minutes. Keep warm.

**5.** Remove the rolls from the heat and allow to cool slightly. Drizzle warm praline sauce on top and serve cinnamon rolls warm.

# HOLIDAY EGGNOG

MAKES ABOUT 6 CUPS

**1.** In a large saucepan set over a propane burner or your stove, cook milk over medium heat until almost boiling. In a large bowl, whisk together eggs and sugar. Whisking constantly, pour hot milk in a thin stream into the egg mixture.

**2.** Put the contents of the bowl into the saucepan and add cream, vanilla, nutmeg, and salt. Cook over low heat, stirring frequently, until temperature reaches 170°F.

**3.** Remove from heat and cool, uncovered, in the refrigerator for at least 2 hours. Stir in bourbon and brandy. To serve, pour chilled eggnog into sparkly glasses and sprinkle with cinnamon.

3 cups whole milk

4 large fresh eggs

1 cup sugar

1 cup heavy cream

1 teaspoon vanilla extract

1/2 teaspoon freshly grated nutmeg

1/8 teaspoon salt

6 ounces bourbon, or to taste

6 ounces brandy, or to taste

For serving: cinnamon

Granny's Pecan Rolls.

1 jigger (1½ ounces) bourbon

1 teaspoon simple syrup

1 teaspoon crème de cacao or chocolate liqueur (chocolate liqueur is slightly sweeter)

2 tablespoons cold-brewed Jay D's Single Origin Coffee, or your favorite medium-roast brand

2 dashes orange bitters

Ice

For serving: orange slice, cherry, and a cocktail straw

# COFFEE OLD FASHIONED

MAKES 1 DRINK

**Consider serving these smooth eye-opener cocktails at your next brunch.**

In an Old Fashioned glass, stir together bourbon, simple syrup, and crème de cacao. Add coffee and bitters, and stir well. Fill glass with ice and stir well again. Garnish with orange slice, cherry, and a cocktail straw. Serve immediately.

# IRISH COFFEE

MAKES 1 DRINK

½ cup hot brewed Jay D's Single Origin Coffee, or your favorite medium-roast brand

1½ teaspoons simple syrup

1 jigger (1½ ounces) Irish whiskey

For serving: whipped cream and cinnamon

In a tall coffee mug, preferably glass, stir together coffee and simple syrup. Stir in whiskey and gently top with as much whipped cream as you like. Sprinkle whipped cream with cinnamon and serve immediately.

# JALAPEÑO RELISH

MAKES ABOUT 1½ CUPS

**I like to serve this relish alongside grilled meats.**

Combine all ingredients well in a metal mixing bowl or in a glass bowl or jar. Cover tightly and store in the refrigerator up to 2 weeks.

6 fresh jalapeños, diced (for milder relish, remove seeds and membranes)

1 medium red onion, diced

½ cup sugar

½ cup apple cider vinegar

1 tablespoon kosher salt

1 teaspoon mustard seeds

1 teaspoon celery salt

¼ teaspoon powdered turmeric

# BARBECUE COMPOUND BUTTER

MAKES 1 CUP

**Try this butter on steaks and grilled seafood, or any savory dish you finish with butter.**

Mix ingredients together in a small mixing bowl. Spoon butter onto parchment paper or plastic wrap and roll into a log. Chill at least 2 hours before serving.

1 cup (2 sticks) unsalted butter, softened

1 tablespoon Jay D's Spicy & Sweet Barbecue Rub (purchased or recipe page 183, or your favorite commercial brand)

# CAJUN SEASONING

MAKES ABOUT ⅔ CUP

3 tablespoons salt

3 tablespoons medium-grind black pepper

1 tablespoon cayenne pepper

1 tablespoon ancho chili powder

1 tablespoon garlic powder

1 tablespoon onion powder

1 tablespoon smoked paprika

There's a ton of commercial Cajun seasoning mixes out there, and most are extremely good. It's also super easy to make your own using ingredients you like.

Mix everything together and store in an airtight container.

# CREOLE SEASONING

MAKES ABOUT 3/4 CUPS

3 tablespoons kosher salt

2 tablespoons granulated garlic

2 tablespoons paprika

1 tablespoon black pepper

1 tablespoon granulated onion

1 tablespoon cayenne pepper

1 tablespoon dried oregano

1 tablespoon dried thyme

My Creole Seasoning focuses more on herbs than the Cajun version. You can certainly buy one at the store, or you can blend your own.

Mix everything together and store in an airtight container.

# HOT CHICKEN SEASONING

MAKES ABOUT 2 CUPS

½ cup cayenne pepper

½ cup light brown sugar

½ cup ground black pepper

¼ cup paprika

¼ cup garlic powder

1 tablespoon salt

I often turn to this seasoning mix when I grill chicken or make hot chicken wings. But be careful with it; too much will make the dish too hot.

Combine all ingredients until mixed evenly. Store in an airtight container.

# JAY D'S SPICY & SWEET BARBECUE RUB

MAKES 2½ CUPS

Mix all ingredients together and store in an airtight container.

½ cup light brown sugar

½ cup ground black pepper

½ cup smoked sweet paprika

⅓ cup chili powder

⅓ cup kosher salt

2 heaping tablespoons garlic powder

2 heaping tablespoons onion powder

3¼ teaspoons cayenne pepper

# COFFEE CHILE RUB

MAKES ABOUT 2½ CUPS

Mix everything together, and store in a glass jar or plastic container at room temperature.

1 cup plus 3 tablespoons Jay D's Single Origin Coffee, finely ground, or your favorite commercial brand

½ cup light brown sugar

¼ cup plus 3 tablespoons chipotle chili powder

3 tablespoons kosher salt

3 tablespoons cumin

2 tablespoons granulated garlic

2 tablespoons granulated onion

2 tablespoons coarsely ground black pepper

1½ tablespoons coriander

# JAY D'S LOUISIANA MOLASSES MUSTARD

MAKES ABOUT 6 CUPS

3½ cups yellow mustard

1¼ cups light molasses

¾ cup Louisiana-style hot sauce

½ cup white sugar

½ cup water

**Light molasses is made from the first boiling of sugarcane juice. It has a milder, sweeter taste than dark molasses, which is made from the second cane juice boiling.**

Combine all ingredients in a saucepan and simmer 20 minutes. Cool completely. Pour into an airtight container, and store in the refrigerator.

# BARBECUE AIOLI

MAKES 1½ CUPS

**Don't let the name of this dipping sauce scare you. Aioli is nothing more than fancied-up mayonnaise.**

Combine all ingredients in a bowl and chill at least 30 minutes. Keeps covered and chilled in your refrigerator up to 1 week.

1 cup mayonnaise

¼ cup Jay D's Louisiana Barbecue Sauce (purchased or recipe page 186, or your favorite commercial brand)

3 teaspoons apple cider vinegar

1½ teaspoons Cajun seasoning (purchased or recipe page 182)

¼ teaspoon garlic powder

# WHITE BARBECUE SAUCE

MAKES 4 CUPS

**This is similar to the white sauce that's favored in the barbecue joints in Alabama. I use it to baste smoked chicken, or to top pulled-pork sandwiches.**

Combine all ingredients until mixed evenly. Transfer to a glass bowl or jar, cover tightly, and refrigerate until ready to use. Keeps up to 1 week in the refrigerator.

3 cups mayonnaise

6 tablespoons apple cider vinegar

¼ cup freshly squeezed lemon juice

4 teaspoons honey

1½ teaspoons cayenne pepper

¾ teaspoon ground black pepper

Kosher salt to taste

# JAY D'S LOUISIANA BARBECUE SAUCE

MAKES ABOUT 9 CUPS

4 cups water

392 grams tomato paste

Dry ingredients:

196 grams brown sugar

12 grams onion powder

9 grams garlic powder

7 grams smoked paprika

4 grams chili powder

4 grams salt

4 grams black pepper

4 grams cayenne pepper

2 grams dried thyme

Wet ingredients:

241 grams Steen's Cane Syrup

112 grams Creole mustard

39 grams Worcestershire sauce

39 grams Cajun-style hot pepper sauce

72 grams apple cider vinegar

63 grams lemon juice

6 grams tamarind concentrate

**Yes, indeed. This is the exact recipe for my commercial barbecue sauce, which is found in stores throughout Louisiana and online. To assure that you get the same distinctive taste I sell in a bottle, use a kitchen scale to weigh out the ingredients in grams.**

**1.** Add water to a large saucepot set over the medium-high heat of a propane burner or your stove. As water is heating, stir in the tomato paste. As soon as the pot simmers, one-by-one, drop in the dry ingredients. To reduce clumping, whisk or immersion blend as spices are added.

**2.** One at a time, whisk in the wet ingredients. Bring the pot to a boil and reduce heat to a simmer. Cook, uncovered, until slightly thick, at least 1 hour, stirring occasionally. Let the sauce cool at room temperature. Store in a covered glass jar in the refrigerator up to 2 weeks.

# PHOTOGRAPH CREDITS

Page vii: Courtesy of Taylor Mathis.

Page ix: Courtesy of Jenn Ocken Photography.

Page x: Courtesy of Phyllis Ducote.

Page xi: Courtesy of Phyllis Ducote.

Page xii: Courtesy of Food Network.

Page xvi: Courtesy of Jennifer Robison.

Page 2: Courtesy of Phyllis Ducote.

Page 4: Courtesy of Jordan Hefler Photography.

Page 5: Courtesy of Taylor Mathis.

Page 7: Courtesy of Jennifer Robison.

Page 8: Courtesy of Jennifer Robison.

Page 9: Courtesy of Fortunato M. Ramin.

Page 11: Courtesy of Maria Do.

Page 12: Courtesy of Frank McMains.

Page 13: Courtesy of Jordan Hefler Photography.

Page 19: Courtesy of Maria Do.

Page 22: Courtesy of Jordan Hefler Photography.

Page 24: Courtesy of Phyllis Ducote.

Page 27: Courtesy of Eric Ducote.

Page 28: Courtesy of Eric Ducote.

Page 29: Courtesy of Phyllis Ducote.

Page 30: Courtesy of Nicole Colvin.

Page 31: Courtesy of Jay Ducote.

Page 32: Courtesy of LSU.

Page 40: Courtesy of Nicole Colvin.

Page 41: Courtesy of Maria Do.

Page 43: Courtesy of Maria Do.

Page 46: Courtesy of Jay Ducote.

Page 47: Courtesy of Jay Ducote.

Page 53: Courtesy of Jordan Hefler Photography.

Page 57: Courtesy of Jay Ducote.

Page 59: Courtesy of Maria Do.

Page 60: Courtesy of Jay Ducote.

Page 62: Courtesy of Frank McMains.

Page 64: Courtesy of Christi Childs.

Page 66: Courtesy of Jordan Hefler Photography.

Page 70: Courtesy of Jordan Hefler Photography.

Page 71: Courtesy of Mike Buck Photography.

Page 72: Courtesy of Mike Buck Photography.

Page 74: Courtesy of Jordan Hefler Photography.

Page 75: Courtesy of Mike Buck Photography.

Page 77: Courtesy of Jordan Hefler Photography.

Page 82: Courtesy of Eric Ducote.

Page 84: Courtesy of Phyllis Ducote.

Page 86: Courtesy of Phyllis Ducote.

Page 88: Courtesy of Jordan Hefler Photography.

Page 95: Courtesy of Maria Do.

Page 99: Courtesy of Blair Loup.

Page 102: Courtesy of Eric Ducote.

Page 103: Courtesy of Eric Ducote.

Page 109: Courtesy of Jordan Hefler Photography.

Page 111: Courtesy of Mike Buck Photography.

Page 114: Courtesy of Mike Buck Photography.

Page 117: Courtesy of Jordan Hefler Photography.

Page 119: Courtesy of Maria Do.

Page 121: Courtesy of Maria Do.

Page 123: Courtesy of Blair Loup.

Page 128: Courtesy of Phyllis Ducote.

Page 130: Courtesy of *MasterChef* on Fox.

Page 137: Courtesy of Frank McMains.

Page 138: Courtesy of Cynthia LeJeune Nobles.

Page 143: Courtesy of Frank McMains.

Page 148: Courtesy of Food Network.

Page 151: Courtesy of Blair Loup.

Page 153: Courtesy of Jordan Hefler Photography.

Page 154: Courtesy of Blair Loup.

Page 156: Courtesy of Frank McMains.

Page 161: Courtesy of Jordan Hefler Photography.

Page 163: Courtesy of Jordan Helfer Photography.

Page 165: Courtesy of Blair Loup.

Page 169: Courtesy of Jordan Hefler Photography.

Page 169: Courtesy of Jordan Hefler Photography.

Page 170: Courtesy of Jeremy Ramsey.

Page 171: Courtesy of Jeremy Ramsey.

Page 173: Courtesy of Richard Hanley.

Page 174: Courtesy of Fortunado M. Ramin.

Page 174: Courtesy of Blair Loup.

Page 174: Courtesy of Frank McMains.

Page 179: Courtesy of Frank McMains.

Page 180: Courtesy of Jordan Hefler Photography.

Page 183: Courtesy of Cynthia LeJeune Nobles.

Page 184: Courtesy of Jordan Hefler Photography.

Page 187: Courtesy of Jordan Hefler Photography.

Index photos: Courtesy of Jordan Hefler Photography.

# INDEX